D1346936

Saira is a suc............, ... s woman, bringing up .... still know nothing of wh... to .... the .... ver ....

Since I'm a successful, independent business woman, bringing up her daughter alone. Her family still know nothing of what she has been through and names have been changed to protect Saba and her daughter from their anger. Should they find out how she has dishonoured them they might very well decide to kill her.

Disgraced

Saira Ahmed
with Andrew Crofts

headline

First published in 2008
by HEADLINE REVIEW

First published in paperback in 2009
by HEADLINE REVIEW

An imprint of Headline Publishing Group

16

Cataloguing in Publication Data is available from the British Library

ISBN 978 0 7553 1818 6

Typeset in Dante by Avon DataSet Ltd,
Bidford-on-Avon, Warwickshire

Printed in the UK by CPI Group (UK) Ltd, Croydon, CR0 4YY

Headline's policy is to use papers that are natural, renewable and recyclable
products and made from wood grown in sustainable forests. The logging and
manufacturing processes are expected to conform to the environmental
regulations of the country of origin.

HEADLINE PUBLISHING GROUP
An Hachette Livre UK Company
338 Euston Road
London NW1 3BH

www.headline.co.uk
www.hachettelivre.co.uk

I would like to dedicate this book to my child and to all the young people who find themselves torn between trying to be good Muslims and finding their own path in life. I hope that reading this story will give hope to those who are feeling trapped by their cultures, their families or their marriages, showing them that it is always worth fighting for what you believe in.

Contents

Contents

Introduction

My family believe that I have disgraced and dishonoured them in many ways since I turned from a girl into a woman, but they know only the tiniest part of the truth. If they ever found out just how I have been living my life for the last few years my brothers would literally kill me, even though I did it in order to support the family financially during difficult times.

By writing this book I hope to explain how it is that a girl who has been brought up to be a strict Muslim and an obedient daughter, sister and wife, can end up having to break every rule in order to survive and help her parents to fulfil their obligations to the wider family. It is the story of a generation caught between two fundamentally opposed cultures, and the story of a girl, like many others, who had to make difficult choices and didn't always get it right.

My choice was whether I was going to live the life that the men in my family wanted me to, or whether I was going to be able to find the courage and the strength to be independent.

1

The First Time

There are two words in Islam which sum up just about everything, 'halal' and 'haram'. Halal means everything that is right and lawful according to the laws of the religion, while haram means everything that is unlawful and wrong.

Even though I had allowed my mind to wander so much during those long hours in the mosque as a child, I knew all too well the difference between the two, and I knew that the path I was now setting out on was haram. But then I knew it was halal for me to help my mother and father to pay off their debts and I could think of no other way to do that. I also knew that many of the traditions of Islam were impractical to live by in a modern, Western society. But still my conscience was heavy as I parked the car and stared at the towering walls of the factory I had been sent to, wondering what fate awaited me inside.

Whatever was going to happen, I now wanted to get it over with as quickly as possible and get out of there with the money that I needed so badly. I rang the telephone number the woman at the escort agency had given me and announced that I was outside.

'I'll let you in,' the man said and a few moments later, when I saw the door open, I got out of the car and walked over, trying to fix a confident smile on my face. I was shocked when I saw him because he was so old he reminded me of my uncle. I suppose in my mind I had imagined he would be young and good-looking, which was a ridiculous thing to expect. I don't know why it hadn't occurred to me that it would often be old men who hired escorts because they would be the ones with the money and the ones who would have less chance of getting a young girl into bed for free. He was obviously the boss because he was smartly dressed in a suit and tie and appeared totally at ease, as if there was no one he had to worry about impressing because I was being paid to be there whether I liked him or not.

He didn't seem to be even slightly embarrassed to be receiving a visit from an escort as he led me across the factory floor in full view of all his workers. In fact it was almost as he was showing me off, flaunting me in front of them. They watched my progress all the way through to his office at the back of the building and I heard a few shouted comments floating out over the roar of the machinery. I could tell they were aimed at me, but couldn't make out the words. The man striding ahead of me showed no sign of having heard anything. If he did he certainly didn't care.

I felt like a complete outsider in this alien world hidden inside high factory walls. But it was a feeling I had grown used to throughout my childhood. It had always felt to me as if everyone else belonged to some wonderful friendship club that I was excluded from and could find no way into. If a party was being arranged at school everyone else would be talking and giggling about it excitedly, but no one would ever think to invite me, perhaps because they knew that my family would never allow me to attend anyway. It was the same when I was at family gatherings. Either it was the men who were all talking and laughing and ignoring the women and girls, or it was the adult women ignoring me as they chattered away about their adult concerns, or it was my brothers ignoring me because I was merely a girl. So, having these men staring at me and shouting comments as if I had no feelings was just one more confirmation of how worthless I was. To me it seemed as if they were all friends, part of a social group, and I was merely an object for their mockery and innuendo. I lifted my head high and stared straight ahead as I marched on, trying to keep up with the long strides of their boss.

I had no idea what I was walking towards as I made my way past their work benches, but I guessed that every one of the men watching knew exactly why I was there. I wished I had never started on the whole adventure. Part of me wanted to turn round and run back to my car as fast as I could, but then I would have had to pass them all again. They would all have seen me running away, which would have been even more humiliating.

The office he showed me into was surprisingly nicely furnished and decorated and when he closed the door behind us it blocked out the worst of the noise from the machines outside. There were big sofas and armchairs and I could see through an open door behind his desk on the other side of the room that he had his own private bathroom and shower. Not knowing what was expected of me, I sat down on one of the chairs and tried to look comfortable and composed. He was staring at me now and smiling. All I wanted to do was get out of that room as quickly as possible, but I stayed rooted to the chair like a frightened rabbit. I could feel sweat breaking through on virtually every inch of my skin and I had to consciously force myself not to shake.

'Oh yes,' he muttered, almost to himself, 'very nice, very nice.'

He came closer, lowered his face towards my neck and breathed in deeply, like he was trying to inhale me. 'You do realise you are wearing too much perfume, don't you? My wife would notice that straight away. She would smell that on me. I've got to be so careful.'

I remembered a comment the girl in the agency had made about me wearing too much perfume and understood now why she had said it. She hadn't actually been trying to insult me, just imparting some professional advice. Maybe, I thought, this was going to be my excuse to escape, or would he make me go for a shower? I hardly dared breathe as I waited for whatever he would say next. He went back to his desk, picked up the phone and rang the agency.

'She's a very pretty girl,' he said when the woman picked up, 'but she's wearing too much perfume. I'm going to have to send her away, but I'm still going to pay her.'

To my amazement he pulled out his wallet and counted out three hundred pounds, which he passed over to me. I realised that I was being dismissed, that this was my chance to get away without having to do anything else. It was as if a mighty weight had been lifted from my shoulders and I sprang out of the chair. I thanked him politely and left the office on my own, walking speedily through the gauntlet of jeers and catcalls, my eyes fixed on the exit sign at the far end.

I burst out into the quiet, cool night air. I was still shaking as I climbed into the car and snapped the locks down. If only I had learned my lesson that night and realised what a narrow escape I had had.

2

Enslaved in Britain

From the moment she arrived in Britain, Mum was treated pretty much as a slave by everyone in my father's family, even by my two brothers once they came along. So when I was born in 1971, nothing much was going to change except that she had one more person to look after until I was old enough to start helping her.

Her own family, which consisted primarily of her parents and her many siblings, were the people who might have stuck up for her, and certainly would have comforted her when things seemed unbearably difficult, were they not all living thousands of miles away in a small village outside Lahore. I doubt if she ever told any of them just how miserable her life was in Britain because she would have known there was nothing they could do. Her fate had been decided the day they agreed she should marry my father and she had to make the best of it. Their lives were hard in many ways too.

She was only seventeen years old when she arrived at Heathrow as a newly married woman with only one spare

9

set of clothes in her luggage (so she could always have one set on and one in the wash) and she would immediately have been put to work by her in-laws. Hard work would not have come as a surprise to her because she was the oldest of five children and was used to performing a mother's endless chores even before she had given birth to children of her own, but still the transition to a foreign land and a family of strangers must have been a shock, requiring her to build a brittle shell over her own feelings in order to protect herself from hurt.

Dad and his family were already established in Britain by the time she arrived. He and his brothers had started a garment factory and were making a living supplying the fashion industry, working every waking hour to produce enough goods to supply the market. The world we all inhabited was self-contained and isolated from the rest of society around us. Most of the women couldn't even speak English and certainly didn't mix with English people. They stayed locked within the confines of the family just as they would have done had they stayed in Lahore, serving their men, their parents and their children.

'Garment factory' makes their family enterprise sound a great deal grander than it actually was. In fact it was all housed in one big backstreet shop premises, with a warehouse room above the shop filled with cutting tables (for the men) and sewing machines (for the women), where every female relative they could round up within a twenty-mile radius worked endless hours to produce denim jackets, skirts and jeans.

Every member of the family was working hard at keeping the business going and to bring in enough money to send home to relatives even harder up than themselves, and they all had barely a moment to spare for household chores like cleaning and cooking, or even making cups of tea. So when Mum arrived, as a vulnerable teenage bride to a much older man, she was immediately set to work by the others, who were anxious to make their own lives easier in any way they could. Because Dad was the youngest of the brothers, Mum gained no status amongst the other women from being his wife. She was the most junior worker there in every sense.

Most of the men who came to the factory to buy were related to us in one way or another, either by blood or marriage. Everyone was someone's uncle or aunt or cousin. Many of them ran shops in other cities around the country and would stock their vans up with the goods that our family made, packing them in as tightly as they could for the long journeys down the motorways, haggling over prices with Dad and my uncles, handing over wads of money or making deals for future payments while the women kept their eyes modestly down on the constantly bobbing needles of their sewing machines.

Dad was twenty years older than Mum and he had his family around him for moral and financial support. She was all alone in Britain, separated from the people she loved the most in the world, her brothers and sisters. I'm told Mum's father was disappointed when he realised what a big age gap there was between his daughter and the man he had promised her to. The photographs he had been shown of Dad by relatives anxious to make the match had been more than ten years out of date, but my grandfather didn't realise he had been duped until Dad and his family arrived for the wedding. By then it was too late and the deal had been done, promises had been made and honour had to be upheld. Mum had to accept her fate without protest and her parents had to be grateful that they had at least found her a husband who would take her to Britain.

Not that Dad was a bad man; he just wasn't able to offer her an easy life because he didn't have one himself. He had been good-looking as a young man, which was why the old photograph had convinced my grandfather that it would be a good match, but he also had an ex-wife, which Mum didn't discover until after she had married him. His first marriage had been arranged by his family as well and had resulted in three children who were already on the way to being grown up by the time he married Mum. The first wife had been chosen for him from among his cousins, and so there was a great deal of ill feeling when Dad announced that he didn't like her any more and wanted to leave her and take a new wife from outside the family, a girl the same age as his own children.

Pakistani men of Dad's generation often marry more than once. If a man's first arranged marriage turns out to be disappointing, which tends to happen in most cases, he will simply find a new wife and move on. A woman has no such escape route, of course; the husband her family chooses for her is the one she is stuck with, unless he dies or divorces her.

My half brothers and sisters were all living around us, both when we were in Britain and when we went back to Pakistan, and many of them worked in the factory. They were polite and respectful to Dad's face, but there was always an undercurrent of bitterness in the air from the members of Dad's first family, all of whom felt that they had been rejected in favour of the pretty teenage second wife. My mother must have felt the hostility towards her from the first day she joined the family and probably put in extra effort initially in order to try to win their approval. Not only were some of her stepchildren the same age as her, but to make things worse she was more beautiful than their mother had ever been, her skin paler and her features finer, making them all the more resentful towards her. Although her looks had won her a husband, they had also made the other women in the family jealous and the men lecherous, many of them giving her what's called 'a bad eye'. Everyone in the family, it seemed, wanted to find a way to put the poor young girl in her place, to make her aware that they were above her in the pecking order.

Mum fell pregnant almost immediately upon arriving in the country but just because she was pregnant she wasn't allowed to lighten up on her other tasks. My eldest brother, Ali, was born about nine months after her arrival and a little over a year later my second brother, Asif, was born. Just over a year after Asif was born, mum gave birth to a stillborn baby girl – something we never really talked about. Two years after that it was my turn to arrive. Still Mum had to work as hard as she could in the house and factory, but now she had three small children to look after at the same time.

Every morning, often before it was even light, a van would travel around from house to house, bundling the women of the family into the back to drive them to the factory, but the women's days started long before that. In our house Mum was expected to get up and prepare breakfast for the whole family, make sandwiches for everyone to take with them to the factory and get us children ready for the day. She wouldn't even have time to wash her own face or comb her hair before she had to clamber into the white van with the rest of the workers. From the age of seven I used to go with her to the factory at weekends and the journeys were always uncomfortable rides. The men would all sit in the front while the women and children perched in the back, on bags of cloth or the wheel arches, desperately trying to keep their balance as they swung round every corner. The only glimpse we would get of the outside world would be from the two almost blacked-out windows in the back doors.

There were only two women at the factory that I can remember who weren't close family members, and even they were related to friends of the family. They would be paid their wages each Friday, but I don't remember ever seeing any of the family members being paid at all for the endless hours they put in.

Once she arrived at the factory Mum would be making tea for everyone and sweeping the floors as well as doing her share of the sewing. At the end of the day she would be taken home again in the van and would start again, cooking another meal for whoever was in the house, while at the same time trying to get my brothers and me washed and ready for bed. There was never a moment when someone wasn't ordering her about or shouting at her, but she kept going, silent and grim-faced, determined to do her duty and not to complain. She had virtually no contact with English people, since Dad, like most Pakistani men, did all the shopping, bringing it home with him in bags and boxes in the evening so she had no reason to make regular journeys outside. Most of the time everyone in the family spoke Urdu or Punjabi around the house and factory so she never became truly fluent in English, always remaining a Pakistani living in a foreign land, but she mastered enough to get by when necessary.

Most parents in Pakistan like to find husbands who will take their daughters to countries like Britain for at least a few years, because they believe there are more opportunities to prosper and enjoy a better life there. Many of the families who emigrated at the time my parents did, did enjoy better standards of living once they had established themselves in more prosperous countries, but for many the cultural clashes they had to endure made life difficult for them in other ways. Although the other family members did treat Mum like a slave, they were all having to work hard as well, both the men and the women. I often remember us all being at the factory until midnight, struggling to fulfil an urgent order. Everyone was striving to keep their head above water, and it was a communal effort, but the strain of surviving left many family members drained and bitter and easily angered with one another. Nerves were always stretched. All the women seemed to like to have someone younger and more vulnerable than themselves to take their spite out on, all the men lost their tempers and bullied whoever they could.

My uncles must have made a reasonable amount of

money during those busy years, but it all disappeared as quickly as it came in. Much of it was sent back to family members still living in poverty in Lahore. For all of them that was considered to be their foremost duty, the reason their families had strived to make it possible for them to travel and live abroad. We all accepted that we had to work every hour that we could in order to support dependent relatives as well as to try to establish comfortable lives for ourselves and for future generations. No one had ever expected anything different of life until the generation that had been brought up in the West, like my brothers and me, began to question some of the rules and traditions that our parents' generation had taken for granted. That was when the cultures started to clash.

We certainly weren't living in poverty, and we knew that because we had seen how our relatives back in Lahore lived. Dad would always buy me new clothes so that I would look pretty when we went out and would be a credit to the family and there was always food on the table, but we never had as much in the way of material goods as other, more Westernised families that we knew.

I don't think Dad ever really knew what was going on with the business; all that was left to my oldest uncle as the senior man of the family. Dad was always treated as the junior partner because he was younger than the others, and he was too respectful to protest when he was left out of decision-making processes. The frustration that he felt at not being in control of his own destiny, however, would often spill out in explosions of temper at his children once his brothers had gone back to their own homes and he could be master in his house for a few hours.

So many times I have heard stories from Asian women of how the older women in families like Dad's treat the young girls their men marry with a total lack of respect or compassion. No doubt they were treated the same way themselves when they were first married off, and maybe their fathers and brothers treated them like servants before that, so I suppose they know no different. In families like ours that is just the way things are for women, so when they are young and inhibited they don't complain, they just do what is asked of them, biding their time until it is their turn to be the elders and the bullies. The men and older women always had to be served first at mealtimes, for instance, which meant that often there was no food left for Mum once she had finished serving up, but she never complained.

Whatever their age, the women in families like ours are nearly always treated thoughtlessly by their men. They are often subjected to physical violence if they try to stand up for themselves, so they have traditionally let the men get away with it. However badly the men in a family might behave, older and more experienced women will always counsel the younger wives to be forgiving.

'At least he comes home sometimes,' they would say. 'At least you have someone to call a husband.'

In the end that was all that mattered because a woman without a husband in the villages of Pakistan would have little hope of thriving. So, once she was married and living in Britain as part of Dad's extended family, there was nowhere Mum could escape to. Her future had been decided and she just had to endure it as best she could.

'Why did you put up with it?' I would ask her when I was older and heard her telling stories about those times.

'I would think of my father,' she said, 'and I didn't want word to get back to him about what a bad wife I was. He had chosen my husband for me and so I had to honour that arrangement. Also, what else could I do? I had no money and I hardly spoke English.'

Dad's eldest brother was the head of the family in Britain, and he ran it with a rod of iron. His family was a lot older than us, his grandchildren being my contemporaries, which meant we were a long way down in the family pecking order. Dad was always a strict husband and father, even when we were alone, but he became a real tyrant whenever Uncle was around, insisting we wore our scarves wrapped tightly around our heads, which I hated. He would make us cut our nails short too, which I always resented. It felt as if he was accusing us of being dirty and not washing our hands properly. My uncle was as strict with his granddaughters as he had been with his daughters, insisting that they left school and did not continue with their studies, even though they had been receiving good academic reports. He was never prepared to compromise on any of his beliefs and we were all too frightened to stand up to him and argue. His wife was enormously overweight and always moaning about pains in her legs and pains in her head, but she somehow found the strength to enforce her husband's rules upon the rest of us. There was always a feeling of resentment in the air among the younger women, who were never able to express their own opinions, or even sit down and have a cup of tea when they felt like it without someone lecturing or bullying them. Perhaps my uncle was afraid that if the women were given too much leisure time to talk they might join forces and stage a rebellion of some sort. He was strict with the boys too, when it came to religious matters, but they had far more personal freedom when it came to going out and pleasing themselves. I think he was hoping they would all grow up to become mullahs and be upstanding members of the Muslim community.

When Uncle came to our house Mum and I and any other females who were there would have to disappear into the kitchen to work while the men sat and talked in the front room. Now that I am a grown-up with a house of my own I like to leave all the doors open between the rooms and I'm sure that is because I used to hate the feeling of being shut away in the kitchen as if we were second-class citizens. We weren't allowed to make the slightest sound, which is virtually impossible when you are cooking and laying out a meal to take through to another room. It was supposed to be as if we weren't there. If we accidentally banged two plates together or dropped cutlery on the work surface Dad would come bursting in, shouting and beating us for showing him up in front of his revered brother.

'You know you must be silent when we have visitors,' he would rage, apparently unable to understand how we could be so careless and ignorant. He was always desperate to impress his brother and to prove to him what a good Muslim family we were and how obedient and respectful his womenfolk and children were. If I or my brothers did the slightest thing wrong he would beat us with his belt, using all his strength to teach us a lesson and to vent some of the frustration that must have been building up inside him as he struggled to maintain his own position in the family hierarchy. There was one time when he kept on beating us all for so long and so hard that the woman from next door came round to plead with him to stop because she could hear it all going on through the connecting wall. That drove Dad to even greater heights of fury.

'Don't you dare come to my house and tell me how to bring up my children!' he roared at her.

If my brothers and I were playing out in the garden with our cousins and we were making a noise the women would come hurrying out to quieten us. 'Keep your voices down,' they would scold nervously, 'don't you realise the men are here? You must be quiet.' Our cousins were all older than us and whenever they came to visit we always ended up in trouble. They would get us to show them where Mum kept the sweets, and then they would steal them and it would be us who would get beaten once they had gone.

Uncle made life a lot harder for Mum by continually reminding Dad that his duties should have been with his first wife because she had been a relative before he married her, and only once she was happy could he marry Mum and provide her with whatever she needed. All the other women in the family disapproved of Dad marrying Mum, but they would never have dared to say it to his face as that would have been disrespectful to a man. So they took it out on Mum instead, or dripped their poison into my young ears, making sure I understood that my mother was only a second wife, that she was a lesser person than their relative, Dad's first wife; that Dad had been wrong to have married Mum. I listened and I was hurt but I didn't really understand what they were talking about. I knew I had other half brothers and sisters, but I didn't understand how such a situation could have occurred or why it should be a matter for so much disapproval.

Uncle was a stern man, obsessed with family pride and honour, using his religion as an excuse for everything he wanted to do. Dad was always in awe of him and constantly being dominated and made to do things that were against his nature. His older brothers and sisters were more like parents to him when he first arrived in Britain, his own parents still being back in Lahore. It was only when Dad grew older and was separated more from Uncle that the softer, kinder side of his nature was able to find its way out. All through our childhood he was striving to prove that he was as good a man as his brother, as upstanding and virtuous and religious as the rest of the family.

Because Mum was pretty and because so many of the men gave her the bad eye there were eventually rumours that she was being unfaithful to Dad with one of his cousins. Without any evidence, Uncle took it upon himself to believe the rumours and to dole out the punishment that such an act demanded. Deciding she had dishonoured his family he beat Mum so hard that she still bears the scars thirty years later. I don't believe for one moment that she was guilty of the crimes she was accused of, and I doubt if Dad believed it at the time either. I suspect my uncle just wanted to flex his muscles and remind all the women what would happen if they brought any disgrace to the family name. I was under no illusions about how important it was to obey and please the men at all times, but being a child I didn't question it, I simply accepted it as the way things were.

3

Back Home in the Village

When I was eight years old everything changed among the adults in the family. Although I never fully understood what happened between them, by staying very quietly in the background and listening to them argue I could piece together a little of what was going on. It seemed that Uncle had run up some terrible debts. I didn't understand what that meant exactly, but I could tell that it was making the other men very angry and the women anxious. Knowing what I know now, I expect he had been sending too much money back to relatives in Pakistan because that seems to be what a lot of immigrants do. Whatever the reason, the business suddenly seemed to be in trouble. They let out parts of the factory to other people, desperately trying to bring in more money to pay off whatever Uncle owed. There were a lot of arguments and raised voices coming from other rooms, but in the end all their efforts were to no avail. The men were unable to save the company, and Dad announced one night that he and Mum were going to be taking us to another city, where they would get jobs and be independent of Uncle and the rest of the family.

Although it was a frightening thought for me as a child to be moving to a new city, without the back-up of our extended family all around, in some ways it was a relief to think we would be away from Uncle's influence. Dad was always more relaxed when he didn't have his big brother looking over his shoulder all the time. For Mum it must have been a wonderful development. The collapse of the family business transformed her life. She still had to work every hour of the day looking after us and the house and taking whatever piecework she could get to earn extra money, but at least she was free of the bullying of the other family members most of the time, and free of Uncle's disapproving looks. There were still family visits to contend with when they would arrive at our new house en masse, demanding hospitality while at the same time continuing to show their contempt for her, but most days she was able to be mistress of her own home. As a result she came out of her shell, but the years of being bullied and worked like a slave had left her bitter and critical of everything that went on, particularly if it was to do with any of us.

Dad got himself a job working in a local petrol station, bringing in just enough money to keep us going. Those were our happiest times as a family because there was no one else interfering with us, and my brothers and I were content, most of the time, to behave like model Muslim children, respectful and obedient, never questioning our elders or the things that they told us. It was like the calm before the storm.

Each week Dad would bring home his wage packet and he and Mum would divide it up together; putting aside ten pounds for fruit and vegetables, ten pounds for meat and so on. At the weekend he would go shopping for everything we would need the following week. That was the traditional division of labour in Muslim families, the women saying what they needed and the men going out to buy it. On Monday morning there would be three little piles of ten and twenty pence coins on the mantelpiece, the exact amounts that my brothers and I needed to take with us to school each day so we could buy the drinks and crisps we craved. Any money that was left over was sent back to the family in Pakistan.

Although we always had enough to eat and keep warm, my brothers and I were aware that we were poor. What we weren't aware of was that Mum and Dad often had to borrow money to send back home to help one or other of their relatives out of a crisis. That was their duty, the way things were traditionally done in a family like ours, but the debts were costing them more than they could afford and trouble that we knew nothing about was brewing in the background.

Fitting in and making friends at my new school was hard because I was used to being part of an extended family network. At my previous school I'd had my cousins and all their friends. Many people had known who I was from the first day I arrived, so I wasn't used to going out and making new friends among a crowd of strangers who already knew one another. I felt like an outsider and I probably looked like one too. Some of the other children did make an effort and invited me to play at their houses after school, but Mum would never allow it because she said Dad wouldn't like it, so soon I stopped asking her for permission and automatically told the other children 'no'. It wasn't long before they gave up asking. I don't know why my parents wanted to keep me so separate from other children – maybe they didn't want me 'infected' with their Western ways. We were never allowed to have friends come to our house either.

There was a white family living on the other side of us who had a little daughter. I used to sit in my room upstairs and watch through the window as she played in the garden outside. She would come round and knock on our door sometimes, asking if I could play with her. Because Mum's English wasn't that good she would ask one of my brothers what she was saying. When they translated, her answer was always the same. 'No, Saira can't come out to play. She's busy with other things.' But I wasn't. I was just upstairs, staring out of the window.

I would occasionally be let out into the back garden, but our Asian neighbours had grown sons and they would come out into their garden to play cricket, which meant I had to be hurried back indoors in case they saw me, and then I would be back at the window watching life go on outside without me.

The first school I went to was a mixed-sex one, so in the beginning my brothers were there. They made sure that I never even considered talking to other boys or playing with them, which isolated me even more. When it was time to go out into the playground one or other of them would be watching me all the time, and if it looked as if I was going to play with a boy, or even speak to one, they would swoop down and separate us, my unappointed moral guardians.

'Why are you talking to that boy?' they would demand to know. 'Haven't you got girl friends you can play with? We're going to tell Dad that you're playing with boys.'

I suspected that if they did I would get a beating, so I obeyed them. I did want to be a good Muslim girl if I could. I suppose my brothers thought they understood what was going on in the other little boys' minds because of what was going on in their own. They were very different to me at school, both of them clever in class and skilful at sport, always winning prizes, which meant they were popular, respected and a little feared; easily able to ensure that none of the boys came near me if they forbade it.

As well as the family visits that we had to endure, once a year there would be a religious festival called Eid al-Adha (Festival of Sacrifice) that we would all have to attend, socialising with all the other uncles and aunts and cousins who were still in Britain. Our family had become a vast network of people, spread out between a number of different cities, all their roots stretching back to Mum and Dad's family members who were still in Pakistan.

The first time I went back to visit the family in Lahore, I had mixed feelings about the trip, partly excitement at the thought of seeing all the places and meeting all the people that I had heard the adults talking about around me, and partly trepidation at the prospect of dealing with an alien culture, one that I knew from experience had strict rules of behaviour which I was afraid I might break by mistake and end up being punished for. Although we did visit Dad's family on that trip, it was Mum's parents that I remember most clearly. That was where we spent most of our time and where I saw a different side to Mum. She seemed completely happy and at home amongst her siblings and I saw that as the older sister she was treated with a respect she never received in Britain. We were only a few days with Dad's family but even to my young eyes and ears there seemed to be a lot of bitterness and bad feeling directed towards us because of Dad having married Mum.

Mum's parents, and some of her brothers and sisters, were still living in the place that had been their home for generations and there seemed to be a lot of love and affection between all the different generations despite the hardships that they had to endure. Grandad looked a thousand years old to me, his back hunched from bearing the weight of the world and his whole body frail from work and worry, but he was still abnormally tall when he stood up on his wobbly old legs, and his skin was very pale, which explained where Mum had inherited her beautiful complexion from.

The family home was a plot of land on the edge of a village, with a small house built from mud standing at each corner. Each house was occupied by a different part of the family, and the generations moved easily around the compound, socialising and supporting one another. Inside the houses there were some small signs of modernity, like solid concrete floors, but there was still no plumbing available and no running water for washing or drinking. There was a much-needed electric fan in one room of my grandparents' house, but in the other there was a fan that still had to be operated by someone pulling on a rope.

The bathroom in the house we stayed in was a plastered room with a tap and a drain against the wall. If you wanted to wash you had to fetch water from a pump outside the house in order to fill a tank which stood above the walls and fed the water down to the tap. There was no ceiling on the room, so whenever I was in there I was terrified that someone mischievous, like one of my brothers, would decide to climb up and look in at me, so I tried to wash myself as quickly and as modestly as I could. There was a wooden door with hooks on the back to hang your clothes on, but there were gaps between the planks of wood, which I was sure people would be trying to see through. Having been taught that modesty was the most important attribute for any girl, I would spend ages arranging my towels and clothes to try to cover up the cracks so that I could be assured privacy from at least one angle, even if there was nothing I could do about the missing roof.

Because of the animals that lived as part of the family there were flies everywhere and I spent the whole four weeks of our stay armed with two fly swatters, fighting my way in and out of the doors through the buzzing swarms. The women would cook our food on a stove with walls made out of mud, their pans standing on top of the open fire (lit with wood collected from the surrounding fields), which my grandmother would spend hours trying to fan into life with a primitive pair of bellows. When I attempted to emulate her the smoke merely billowed into my face, making my eyes sting and filling my nose and throat. The curries and chapattis they prepared were the same as we had at home, despite the different cooking methods, which was comforting. There was a big, twisted old tree in the courtyard bearing fruit I had never seen in Britain, which we were allowed to pick and eat when we were hungry. It tasted sour and sweet at the same time.

The women would wash their clothes on the banks of the little river that ran alongside the main road through the village, beating the dirt out of them on planks of wood. The river water was thick with the red mud that bonded labourers, encrusted in the red dust, baked into bricks in the many kilns that stood along the sides of the main road into Lahore, exactly as they must have done for hundreds of years. Resting water buffaloes would wallow in the water with just their nostrils, horns and humps showing above the surface as the village children dived in around them, everyone trying to keep cool. I tried swimming once, wading into the river in all my clothes like the other girls, but the water was so dirty it tasted bad and I didn't want to do it again. There was a giant pump in the fields, bringing up water from the ground, which was then distributed over the crops. The men would go down there when they wanted to wash, standing under the fresh cold water.

There were hardly any cars in the village, most of the people travelling to and from the local bus station on carts made of planks of wood on wheels, towed by pairs of donkeys. The village boys would jump on and off the carts as they were trotted around, the drivers standing up on steady legs, constantly trying to whip their tired and thin-looking animals to move faster, laughing and shouting greetings to everyone they passed. I never managed to achieve the village boys' easy agility. Whenever I needed to go anywhere I would always struggle to get on and off the rickety platforms, and then would sit there, clinging on for dear life as the wheels below crashed through every pothole and sprayed the dirt and mud up around me.

Every road was lined with stalls selling fruit and drinks and anything else anyone could get their hands on. Everyone needed to make whatever money they could each day, just to survive, even if it was no more than a few rupees. Since there were no fridges, everything the traders needed to keep cool would be stood on giant blocks of ice. Even if they stood in the shade the heat would turn the blocks into mud puddles by the end of the afternoon.

By the time of my next visit to my grandparents a couple of years later they had built a latrine trench in a hut outside the house. There were planks placed across the ditch that you could stand on, hovering over gaps that allowed the waste to drop down into the hole they had dug below. It was better than having to do your business in the open fields, but the stench was terrible from the results of everyone else's visits that were just lying below the hole in the planks. I can still remember the smells of that house as I hurried past the manure from the buffaloes and the stench of the latrines to get inside, where I was then greeted with the aromas of smoke and cooking from the open fires that burned in the courtyard. Inside the small crowded rooms there would be a mixture of scents from sweating bodies and the many different herbs and spices the women used.

Despite the physical discomforts it was an exciting place for a child to visit and life was not as difficult as I had imagined it would be when we first arrived. I felt that I fitted in amongst the various generations of women, I had a natural place which I wasn't so certain I had in England. I suspect if my parents had never moved from Pakistan I would have married and stayed in a village like that all my life, and my brothers would have become decent, poor, hard-working men. But because our parents tried to improve the lot of the whole family by moving to another culture we were offered glimpses of alternative lifestyles and given access to choices that should have led to us enjoying better lives, but would ultimately lead all three of us down the wrong paths in our life journeys. My uncle would probably have said we were corrupted by the decadent West.

4

Fat and Ugly

Religion played a big role in our family lives all through my childhood and although I found a lot of it boring, I never questioned any of the things I was taught. Every day my brothers and I would come home from school at about three-thirty and have something to eat. By four-thirty or five o'clock we would be in a mosque learning the Qu'ran and the prayers, the rituals of our faith and the Arabic alphabet. I wouldn't look forward to any of it but I didn't think anything was unusual because it was what I believed everyone had to do. The teacher would instruct us to keep on reading the same passages over and over again and I would sit with the book open in front of me, staring at the words, my finger moving back and forth as if I was following the lines and my mind wandering off in a hundred different directions.

My brothers were much more studious about the faith. They knew much more about it than I did as a result, and they knew exactly how to enforce the rules upon me, the girl of the family. It wasn't that I didn't believe in it all, because I did, I just had other things I would have preferred to be doing or thinking about when I was out of school. My inattention made me feel permanently guilty for being a bad Muslim.

A Pir, which is the name in Islam given to a holy man, who was known to our family in Pakistan would come to Britain once a year, and he would travel around, staying a few days in turn with each branch of the family. When he was in our house we women and children were only allowed to appear before him if we were summoned for prayers and teachings, we had to stay hidden from his sight the rest of the time in order to show him respect both as a man and a religious elder. I remember watching him arrive at our house, peeking out through the net curtains upstairs as he climbed out of the car to be greeted by my father at the door. It seemed to me that he actually had a glow of holiness about him as he came into the house with everyone dancing attendance on him. He seemed such a powerful, charismatic man with his long white beard and peaceful manner, that I never questioned the idea that he and the other men were somehow higher up in God's eyes than we mere women would ever be.

As long as he was staying with us everything in the house revolved around his needs and Dad and the boys were demoted to being his acolytes. Mum would make him mountains of special food, eight or ten courses at a time, delicacies that we would never normally be able to afford, and other people in the area would come to our house to pay their respects and listen to his wisdom being dispensed. He would even hold classes for us children while he was there, which we had to attend, obeying all the same rules as when we went to prayers.

I was used to going through all the required rituals of washing and praying five times a day and had learned to short-cut them most of the time. There was a strict routine for the washing; first the private parts, then rinsing out your mouth, your nostrils, your face and inside your ears, and then washing your hands up to the elbows and your feet, everything done three times. It was tedious and time-consuming, and like any normal child I would try to cut corners, running the tap noisily if no one was watching and just pretending to wash, or letting my mind wander when I was supposed to be reading the holy text. The one time I skipped the washing ritual when the Pir was there, however, he knew, although I never understood how. At the end of the class he gently enquired if I had done what I should have done, making my face burn with guilt. Dad slapped me hard afterwards for showing such disrespect to a man who was honouring our family just by being there.

Even after we moved away from the influence of his brothers, Dad was still strict with us about things like keeping up appearances around other members of the family, and if he ever caught us lying he would beat us or give us some other punishment, like making us stand on one leg or facing into the corner of the room, for hours. Mum wasn't quite so vindictive most of the time, but as I grew older she showed her disapproval of me in more and more ways, particularly when it came to my appearance, which seemed to cause her endless frustration – as if she feared she would never be able to marry me off success-fully. She had been so pale and so pretty when she was a girl, but I had inherited Dad's darker colouring, which to her eyes made my skin look dirty all the time. Compared to her and my brothers I was the ugly duckling of the family. The way she would talk to me always made me feel that I was an outsider in the family and so I would do small things to try to feel a bit more loved and cared for. I would tell little lies, like announcing that I felt ill or had toothache or needed my eyes tested, when there was nothing wrong with me at all, just in order to get Mum's attention.

When I did get attention, however, it wasn't always how I wanted it to be. She would insist on bathing me herself, for instance, even when I was a teenager and far too old for such things, telling me that I didn't scrub hard enough to get the dirt off. I had grown breasts and started my period and still she insisted on washing me herself. It felt so unfair because I knew I did wash myself properly. It was just the pigment of my skin that made it look as if I didn't, particularly the dark skin on my neck and throat. She was always accusing me of putting on weight as well because I wasn't stick-thin like her and like so many other girls we knew. The assumption seemed to be that if I were fairer-skinned and slimmer I would stand a better chance of winning a good husband, which was the only ambition anyone in the family had for me.

Over the years I have discovered that it is normal for families like ours to look on girls purely as marriage material. Things had always been that way and only the most forward-thinking immigrant parents seriously believed their daughters should have careers to match their abilities, or even to match the aspirations of their brothers. All a girl was expected to do was find a man who would provide for her and for however many children they might have together. If he could be persuaded to love her and be kind to her as well, that would be a bonus.

If that is all a woman is considered to be good for, however, and she doesn't get a decent education, it leaves her at a severe disadvantage when she does finally get into a marriage. From the moment of the wedding she is completely dependent on her husband and unable to assert herself for fear of being beaten or, worse still, cast aside and left to struggle on her own with no qualifications or skills with which she can earn more than the most meagre of incomes. All of a mother's energies, therefore, have to be concentrated on making her daughters attractive to the right sort of men, which includes keeping them pure and their reputations spotless, and then ensuring that a successful match is made for them.

'You are fat and dirty and you smell,' Mum would tell me as she scrubbed away at me painfully in the bath and I longed to be beautiful and pale-skinned and desirable as she had been when she was my age.

In my heart I believed she must be right because I didn't feel comfortable in my body, particularly as I entered puberty. I was putting on weight and as I transformed into a woman I grew breasts that needed the support of a much better bra than anything Mum was ever going to be willing to buy me. She refused to take me with her when she went out to buy bras for me and so they never fitted, but she didn't seem to care. She wouldn't allow me to use any deodorant under my arms either, so at school I gained a reputation among the other children for having body odour, particularly when we had been doing anything physical like P.E., and there were plenty of girls who were happy to point it out to me.

'Are your parents so poor they can't even buy you a can of deodorant, then?' they would taunt.

The more confident and popular girls would all be squirting themselves under the arms in the changing rooms afterwards but I was too shy to ask them if I could borrow their sprays. The worst smell emanated from my feet. They always seemed to be sweaty and everyone complained about them, both at school and at home, particularly when I took my trainers off. Mum would accuse me of not washing them properly before prayers, so I would scrub and scrub at my feet in an attempt to defeat the sweat glands, but the moment I pushed them back into the cheap trainers Mum insisted on buying me they would start to sweat again. In the end Dad became so desperate he took me to see the doctor.

'Just buy her a decent pair of leather shoes, Mr Ahmed,' the doctor told him, 'so that her feet can breathe.'

To his credit Dad did do as he suggested, and things got a lot better after that, but by that time the damage to my self-confidence had been done and I was paranoid about every tiny odour my body might produce. I longed to be able to wear perfumes and body sprays like all the other girls, who seemed so dainty and fragrant and perfect as I lumbered around them in my cheap clothes and uncut hair, which Mum insisted had to be oiled in the traditional way. Not having any older sisters to learn from I knew nothing about the modern life of other girls, which marked me out even more as an outsider at school whenever I opened my mouth to speak.

'Oh, you are using surma,' I said admiringly one day when I saw one of the other girls darkening her eyes.

Surma is a kind of soot that provides the smutty stain that traditional Asian women rub around their eyes, both for cosmetic effect and because they believe it has magical and healing effects.

'No,' the girl said, looking at me as if I had just landed from another planet. 'It's eyeliner.'

I couldn't imagine how she could ever have talked her mother into allowing her to use such a daring and mysterious product. All Mum possessed was a single lipstick, which she smeared around her mouth about twice a year for special occasions, and there was only one big bottle of baby lotion in the entire house, which we were all supposed to share as a moisturiser.

'Why can't I wear skirts like them?' I would ask Mum as we walked home behind groups of fashionably dressed girls, who all seemed to be laughing and gossiping together about subjects that were a complete mystery to me.

'No,' she would say in a voice that meant the subject wasn't open for discussion. 'You don't want to be like them.'

I was too closed in on myself and too shy to be able to thrive in the competitive atmosphere of any school. It felt to me as if the whole world was against me. Mum and Dad always seemed to be angry or disapproving of me, and my brothers were always picking on me just like the girls at school. I don't remember ever experiencing the emotion of love in those early days. I didn't expect it, because it wasn't something I had seen around me, so I didn't miss it. I never saw Mum or Dad showing one another the slightest sign of affection. They certainly would never have kissed or touched in front of us. I never even saw them sharing a bed, although they must have done at some time to produce the three of us. Mum would always sleep downstairs on the sofa or in my room with me.

Years later, when I was old enough to talk about such things and when my brothers and I had all left home, I asked Mum why she didn't share a bed with Dad now, just in order to be more comfortable at night.

'Oh no,' she said, apparently shocked by the very suggestion, 'your father never liked that. I've never done that in my life, do you think I am going to start now?'

All the other girls in my classes seemed more open and confident than I could ever dream of being. The only rule about uniform was that we had to wear dark blue clothes. The others were all allowed to choose whatever they wanted and could wear skirts if they preferred. Mum and Dad would only allow me to wear traditional clothes that Mum or another relative had sewn for me, with baggy trousers under a loose tunic. To make things worse the yards of material round my legs would inflate on windy days like parachutes, making me look even huger than I was as I wandered around the playground trying to find someone who would be willing to be my friend.

The vast majority of the children at our schools were Muslim and from Pakistan, but it was obvious from watching them that not all of them were from families as strict as ours. At my second school a lot of the girls were even allowed to walk home from school without their parents chaperoning them. There were others like me who had to wear scarves round their faces, but even they had nicer clothes and more freedom than I did. I used to watch the pretty, popular girls and long to be part of their group. I would try in my shy way to strike up a friendship with them, but I couldn't keep up with their chatter because I hardly ever knew what they were talking about. They would want to discuss television programmes like *Dallas*, *Neighbours* or *Top of the Pops*, which we were never allowed to watch. All we were allowed to watch were kids' programmes or cartoons or educational programmes like *Countdown*, which we had to sit in front of with pens and paper at the ready. If we got the answers right we would be Dad's favourite for the day, but if we got them wrong we 'had no brain' and 'hadn't been concentrating at school'. It never seemed to occur to him that the people answering the questions on the television were adults, not children.

Mum and Dad would bring home Bollywood or Pakistani films sometimes, but even then they would fast-forward them if there were any scenes they considered inappropriate for us to see, like couples singing together or kissing.

P.E. classes were particularly painful for me because Mum still refused to buy me proper bras and my breasts would swing around uncomfortably and unattractively as I ran. I would try to clench them together with my arms, making me move like an awkward middle-aged woman rather than a young girl, making the others laugh and run around behind me imitating me. Their laughter cemented the idea in my own head, as well as in theirs, that I was comical and grotesque. My form teacher, Mrs Thomson, was a kind, no-nonsense sort of a woman and she would tell the other girls off for mocking me, but the damage to my self-confidence had already been done. I started skipping P.E. whenever I could and Mrs Thomson noticed. She called me into her office.

'Is there a problem at home?' she asked.

'No,' I lied. I would have loved to ask her to go to Mum and say that I needed to have deodorant like the other girls, or a proper bra, but I knew Mum and Dad would both go mad and beat me if they ever thought I had been talking to someone outside the family about private matters. It was so rare for anyone to stick up for me that I was impossibly grateful to Mrs Thomson. I never forgot that moment when she had shown some concern for me, whereas my parents showed nothing but contempt.

The secondary school I had been sent to was an all girls'

school and by that time my brothers were allowed to take themselves back and forth to their school on their own, but I still had to be chaperoned every day on the mile-and-a-half walk each way. Either Mum or Dad would always be with me, never allowing me to go on my own. As my brothers got older they were sometimes asked to act as my chaperones if they had come out of school early, and they were just as fiercely protective of me as they had been at our first school, never allowing me to talk to anyone, insisting I go straight home with them so that I wouldn't be corrupted or led astray by any of the other boys, who would be hanging around in cars outside the gates, trying to talk to the girls as they emerged. Many of the other Muslim girls were treated with the same amount of care as I was, so I didn't feel like I was the only one, but still there were some girls who were allowed to walk home themselves and that seemed very mature and glamorous to me. They were the same girls who sometimes jumped over the school fences during the day and went to buy themselves sweets and cigarettes from the local shops. I couldn't imagine how anyone ever found the courage to be so rebellious and I envied their nerve. There was one girl who used to wear a T-shirt with the slogan 'Sex contains no calories' on it.

'What does that mean?' I asked as I read it, unable to contain my amazement, even if it did give away my naivety.

'Well, you don't put on weight if you do it,' she said, looking at me as if I was a complete idiot. 'Do you?'

I spent a lot of time trying to puzzle that one out, not having the faintest idea what any of it was about.

As the boys grew older, Mum and Dad were willing to leave us alone in the house with them in charge. I dreaded those days, because the moment the door closed behind Mum, Ali and Asif would want to play games, which usually seemed to involve me being blindfolded and spun round repeatedly before being locked under the stairs, in the dark, for their entertainment. Ali liked to light matches, puff them out and then stab my face with the smouldering black ends, just to watch me jump and hear me squeal. I still have one or two scars left from that particular game. To me it seemed natural that they would want to pick on me as I was so used to being told that I was inferior because I was dark-skinned, smelly and overweight, but that didn't mean I liked it. They always wanted to play hide-and-seek the moment we were left alone as well, which sounded innocent enough, but it was always me who had to hide and whenever they found me their hands would be all over me, exploring and pinching my boobs and my bum and going up in between my legs. Even though there were only about half a dozen places to hide in the whole house, including the cupboard where they liked to lock me up, they managed to turn the hunt into an exciting sport for themselves and a terrifying ordeal for me every time. I would be able to hear them approaching my hiding places, deliberately taking their time and pretending to search in places they knew I couldn't fit into just to prolong the agony. As soon as they found me and started their rough-and-tumble I would be terrified that they might be going to do something really bad, and I would try desperately to fight them off, struggling not to cry as I begged them not to do it, not wanting to show my weakness and let them know how badly they were frightening me.

It didn't feel right that they should be touching me so invasively and painfully. I could tell that it excited them in a way that was sinful, but I didn't know what I was doing wrong that was making them willing to hurt and degrade me in this way. Was I leading them on? Was it because I didn't cover myself up enough around the house? Was it because I didn't say my prayers well enough or because I longed to wear skirts? To them it was probably no more than a mixture of curiosity and misdirected lust, but I became scared every time I knew that Mum and Dad were going to be out of the house at the same time. I would beg Mum to stay or to take me with her, without being able to explain why I was so afraid, but she never picked up on my desperation, dismissing it as mere foolishness, assuring me there was nothing to fear because my brothers would be there to protect me if anything happened.

One time I was sitting at my window upstairs watching the boys next door playing cricket when my eldest brother came in and caught me.

'You're flirting with those boys,' he said, triumphantly. 'I'm going to tell Mum and Dad what you're doing unless you do what I tell you.'

In order to buy his silence I had to take my top off and show him my breasts and let him grope them, and I had to kiss him on the lips.

'Like they do on the television,' he said.

God knows how he knew what they did on television because I'd never been allowed to see. I suppose he had been able to watch things at his friends' houses when he went round to visit after school.

I don't think I was unusual in keeping silent about such shameful and personal things. Few girls from families like mine would ever have dared to speak up, afraid that they would be blamed for leading the boys on, frightened of incurring the anger of their parents and the disapproval of everyone else, of being branded as impure goods. The embarrassment of speaking of such things would be too much to contemplate, it was infinitely preferable to keep it all inside your head. Perhaps if I had had a better relationship with Mum I would have felt I could speak up, but she never made me feel that I was special in any way, so I assumed that all I deserved was to be groped and pinched and beaten.

Sometimes I wondered if Mum knew more than she let on. There was one night when for some reason I had been put into the same bedroom as Ali and he started trying to kiss me. I pushed him off angrily.

'Please, please let me do it,' he begged, his hands all over me.

'No,' I felt bold, knowing Mum and Dad were downstairs. 'If you try again I will shout for Mum.'

I suppose he didn't believe that I would dare because he kept pressing himself on me.

'Mum!' I shouted, 'Mum!'

The few seconds that it took Mum to come upstairs in answer to my call must have seemed like an age to Ali. He must have felt certain that he was about to be seriously beaten.

'Mum,' I said when she came into the room. 'I don't want to sleep in this room.'

She didn't question it, she simply arranged for me to move to another room immediately as if she knew exactly why I was asking and didn't want to hear the reason put into words that would inevitably lead to terrible consequences. A girl's reputation and honour were even more important than her beauty or her wealth when it came to marrying her off. Any suggestion that I might be impure could ruin all the family's hopes of making a good match for me in a few years' time.

Because of this cloak of silence that shrouds such matters, boys and men in families like ours can get away with anything as long as no one catches them in the act. There is no way of knowing how widespread such things are, but I suspect my experience is more common than most Muslim men would care to admit. Girls from traditional Muslim backgrounds are always guarded assiduously by the men in their families when they are in the outside world, but they are not always protected from the guards themselves when they are young.

Although I didn't like it when they behaved like that, I was always eager to please my brothers in other ways, and was easily led astray by them if I thought it would make them like me more.

'Go and take fifty pence from Mum's handbag,' they would coax and I would obey after only the smallest amount of resistance. Not that I wasn't capable of slipping the odd coin into my pocket of my own accord if I saw the chance. Mum used to ask me to check how much credit we had on the gas meter in the house to see if we needed to feed any more coins into it. I would come back and tell her that it needed fifty pence more than it did, keeping one of the coins for myself. I would then use my ill-gotten gains to buy sweets the next day so that I could hand them round in class in an attempt to make myself more popular. I felt guilty about it at the time, and still do even today, but I was desperate to make people like me and I couldn't think of any other way to do it.

Mum also relented in the end about allowing me to buy a body spray, and I smothered myself in clouds of the stuff. It felt so good to smell fresh at last and not to be constantly having to avoid getting close to other people, but it was too late to undo the damage that had already been done to my reputation. I was known as a fat, smelly, unattractive and boring girl and they were never going to see me any other way, however hard I tried.

Sometimes one of the other girls at school would be sweet and talk to me and my hopes of popularity would soar, but as soon as her real friends turned up she would be off again and I would be left on my own, trying to look as if I wasn't bothered. One of them told me that another girl's brother had said he thought I looked 'nice'. My heart actually quickened as I took in her kindly meant words. A boy thought I was attractive? Which boy? Where was he? What did he look like? Every day for weeks after that I would crane my head around the crowds at the school gates in the hope of seeing some handsome young man collecting his sister while shooting me admiring glances, but I never managed to identify him. No one was looking at me as far as I could tell, certainly not any boys, but that one casual comment brought me so much excitement and gave me a sliver of anticipation that maybe I was going to blossom into a swan at any moment and that more boys would start to show an interest. What a wonderful dream that is when you have been told all your life that you are fat, dirty and unattractive. In the privacy of my own thoughts I would imagine him coming up to talk to me, or maybe asking my father if he might come and visit the house. I would imagine how I would dress and how I would modestly lower my eyes and maybe glance up at him flirtatiously now and then.

But he never showed or declared himself and perhaps it was just as well. I expect the boy that I imagined him to be was far more glamorous and gallant than the real teenage boy would ever have been. Often the life we imagine is so much better than the reality. So I remained the fat, dark-skinned and smelly girl that no one was interested in, and the yearning I felt to be attractive and loved by men smouldered on silently inside me, waiting for the day when it would become too powerful to resist and would burst out, leading me terribly astray.

5

A Potential Husband

Even once my brothers and I were old enough to look after ourselves for much of the time, Mum's life at home was still divided between cooking, cleaning, looking after the men and sitting at the sewing machine which was perm-anently installed in our front room, turning out endless pairs of jeans and denim skirts. It was normal to hear that machine whirring away until three or four o'clock in the morning if you had to get up to go to the bathroom, and Mum would still be back up in order to get us out of bed and ready for school a few hours later. She was always blank-eyed with weariness and easily irritated by everything and everyone. I never remember hearing her laugh or seeing her being joyful, there always seemed to be something for her to be angry about.

She and I never really had the sort of mother-daughter relationship that I could see other girls had. She never did things like help me make pretty hairstyles for myself, just lacing my hair with coconut oil every morning, tying it in two pigtails and fastening the bottoms of them with brown rubber bands that she got free with the groceries. Many of the other girls had their hair styled with gel and hairspray and were given pretty slides and hair bands to wear. She made all my clothes for me, either by cutting down her old clothes so that they more or less fitted me, or making them up from scraps of fabric left over from my uncle's factory.

Eventually Dad relented about my hair and allowed me to get it cut. Almost beside myself with excitement, and imagining just how transformed and beautiful I would be when I came out of the salon, I went to a hairdresser and asked her to give me a fringe. The problem was that the moment I got back outside it went all frizzy and didn't look in the least bit like the sophisticated image I'd had in my mind. I tried to put it up in a ponytail for school the next day, which left two flaps hanging down each side like a spaniel's ears. Instead of looking more like the fashionable girls at school whom I admired so much, I earned a new nickname from them: 'Dumbo'. I was close to despairing of ever being able to make myself look more attractive.

Mum would never sit beside me and say anything loving; there was always a sense of resentment in her voice which I could never understand. I longed to feel wanted and not to be scolded every time she opened her mouth. As my brothers turned into handsome young men I seemed to remain the black sheep of the family. She was so proud of her boys, never believing they could put a foot wrong. In a traditional Muslim family like ours the men and the boys are the most important people at all times and in all situations. Everything had to be done for my brothers before it was done for me. They would always be fed first at mealtimes and they would never be expected to help with the clearing up afterwards, or any other household chores. They were like little princes, and Mum and I were their uncomplaining servants. It wasn't an unusual situation, it was the norm where we came from, and although I thought it was unfair I didn't bother to speak up because I knew there was no point and it would only result in my getting a beating.

Although they were treated as superior to me, the boys received their fair share of punishments when they were small as well. Dad was particularly ferocious about always telling the truth and if he ever caught any of us lying he would beat us as hard as he could. Sometimes he seemed to take pleasure in the punishments, thinking up new humiliations for us. Punishments were always designed to heap as much shame on to the culprit as possible. There were several occasions when one or other of my brothers was in trouble and would be standing in his underpants in the middle of the sitting room, shivering with a mixture of cold and fear, and Dad would call me into the room.

'Hit him,' he instructed me the first time it happened.

Not wanting to hurt my brother for fear of later

recriminations and because such an act seemed to go against all the rules of respect that I'd had beaten into me, but not wanting to disobey Dad and bring his wrath down on to my head either, I administered a slap on his bare legs, but even that made him hiss with pain as he forced himself not to cry.

'No,' Dad roared, producing a bamboo cane and hitting me across the back with all his strength, the impact knocking me off my feet, 'like that!'

He kept on hitting me and making me try again with the cane until he was satisfied that I was delivering my blows as hard as he wanted and my brother had collapsed on to his knees, weeping and begging for mercy. After the first time I always knew what was expected of me when he called me in. Although I don't think my brothers ever blamed me, because they could see that I was being forced to do it against my will, it certainly hardened them towards Dad. Such punishments always seemed too extreme, as if he was trying to work out his own frustration and anger at the way life was treating him rather than trying to guide my brothers or me towards bettering our behaviour. Maybe deep down he believed he was giving us certain morals and rules to live by, fulfilling his duty as a father, but just didn't know how to express himself properly, always choosing to shout and hit rather than sit down and talk.

Although she wasn't as violent, Mum could be strict too if she lost her temper, and she would never intervene on our behalf if our father was punishing us, believing that Dad was always right in the way that he disciplined us, convinced that we needed to learn the same lessons that they had been taught when they were our age. She would shout at us herself if we did anything she thought was wrong. Sometimes she would grab one of us by the wrist and drag us to the cooker, holding our hands over the naked gas flames until we could feel the heat burning our flesh, threatening to press them closer if we didn't behave and obey. Sometimes she would use a hot iron as a weapon, pressing it against our arms or legs, leaving scald marks. Like the older women who persecuted her when she was young, she always seemed to be angry and bitter about everything, quick to find fault with us and to complain that we were making her life even more difficult. We, in turn, were just as docile and accepting of it all as she had been when she first arrived in Britain – at least we were when we were young, but things would change as we grew older and became more aware of the Western way of life that was going on all around us. Maybe Mum and Dad hoped that their discipline would make us strong enough to resist the temptations that they knew would be bound to come before us as we grew up, but if that was their hope it was sadly mistaken.

Whatever their motives, it's possible that by punishing us all so brutally when they were angry, Mum and Dad hardened us in some way, perhaps sowing the seeds of a bitterness and dissatisfaction with life that sent my brothers off down such a wrong and destructive path and later caused me to make a decision that very nearly ruined my life forever. At the same time perhaps they lit a spark of rebellion and developed a toughness in me that was the reason I was able to survive the ordeals that were to come.

Many of the other girls at school were now considered old enough by their families to walk back and forth on their own and I envied them so much. I would watch them talking and laughing and wonder why I could never feel like that. I never really laughed, not from the bottom of my heart. The best I could manage was a sort of nervous giggle. Some of the other girls at school who, like me, had trouble mixing socially made up for it by being clever in class, by putting in extra hours of homework when the others were watching television or socialising and by attaining high grades in their exams. I didn't score there either. I just didn't seem to be able to muster enough self-confidence to go anywhere in any of the subjects I was studying. I never seemed to be able to concentrate in class for long enough to retain the knowledge that the teachers were trying to impart. I would always go into the classroom at the beginning of each lesson meaning to concentrate, and each day I would tell myself that I must try harder, but somehow my mind would almost immediately wander on to the many things that were puzzling and worrying me about life.

The only classes that I really enjoyed and excelled at were art. There had been one particular art teacher who had inspired me when we did a project on textile design. She had allowed us to have a free rein to design whatever we wanted and I did a range of patterns for saris and skirts, the sort of things I would have liked to wear myself. One day she asked me to stay after class and went through my pictures with me standing beside her.

'These are really good, Saira,' she told me. 'I think you have a real talent. Perhaps you should apply to go to art school.'

Her words of praise made my spirits soar, even though I didn't think there was any chance Dad would ever allow me to do such a thing. If he didn't approve of the other girls at my school, he certainly wouldn't approve of the sort of bohemian students who went to art school. Her words of praise still encouraged me and whenever I could get hold of any art materials I would constantly be doodling new patterns, and sketching how they would look as dresses or curtains or cushion covers. I was always completely relaxed and happy when I was absorbed in my patterns and colours.

When it was time to take my GCSEs I think I ended up getting four Cs, one B, one D and one E. Not exactly a glittering educational achievement, but then I had no expectation of ever needing good exam results because I didn't imagine Dad would allow me to go on to further education or to apply for the sort of job that would need academic qualifications. No one else in the family ever suggested that I should think differently. All the women had laboured as seamstresses or shop assistants, nearly always working for other family members, so they had never needed to go to interviews and show anyone any qualifications. I knew there was an alternative path to follow, which was where the more Westernised girls were heading; I just didn't think it was going to apply to me. I wondered if perhaps I could work in one of the garment factories in our area, and then I could show some of my designs to the owners and perhaps they would buy them, turn them into a reality and then hire me to do more. I knew deep inside me that it was a wild dream, which was why I didn't dare to mention it to anyone else for fear of being ridiculed. So I just continued to do my scribbling in private, hiding my sketchbooks if ever anyone else was around, not wanting to have my fragile dreams mocked in case they were destroyed forever.

To be fair to Dad, he would say that he believed I should get an education just like my brothers so that I could be independent when I grew up. He was always willing to buy any books that I needed for revision, but the evidence of my eyes told me that however much he might champion education in theory, in reality we were not the sort of family that believed in equal opportunities for women. Many years later I would ask Dad how he could justify the way that the women in our family were treated by the men, including him, if he truly believed I should be independent when I grew up.

'No matter how we treat our own women,' he said, after a few moments' thought, 'I wouldn't want any man outside the family treating my daughter badly. I would want her to have the education to protect herself.'

He didn't seem to see that there was anything strange in taking such a hypocritical stance, given that he would later hand me over completely to a man who would treat me badly. On the contrary, it seemed to him as if it was obvious that his was the correct way to behave, the only way open to him.

In fact most of his efforts were wasted anyway as I just didn't seem to be able to shine at school, no matter how much I wanted to. I suppose I could have made more of an effort to concentrate in class and improve my exam results in order to prepare myself for real life outside the family, but I was more comfortable living in my own little dream world, and the constant nagging and explosions of anger that went on at home did nothing to change that, making me withdraw further and further inside my head and into my own thoughts. It all seemed pointless anyway. I couldn't imagine that someone as fat and ugly and stupid as I was convinced I was would ever amount to anything in the outside world. In my gloomiest moments I had resigned myself to the idea that I would probably marry some unfortunate-looking man, have children and look after my home and family just like Mum had had to, and like all my aunts and female cousins. Then maybe one day I would have daughters or daughters-in-law who would have to wait on me hand and foot. That, I assumed, would be my destiny and there was little point harbouring any other dreams or ambitions. The idea didn't particularly horrify me, because it was just the way things were likely to turn out, but it certainly didn't bring me any hope or joy either.

The biggest problem I could see was how I was going to win a nice man as a husband when I was so lacking in physical attractions. Every so often a letter would arrive from Pakistan and a photograph of a self-conscious-looking boy or young man who was in need of a wife would fall out on to the kitchen table when Mum opened the envelope.

'What do you think of this one then?' she would ask, holding the latest suggestion up for my inspection, and I would mumble some sort of non-committal answer, not ready yet to even contemplate the possibility of being someone's wife, while at the same time nurturing wildly romantic ideas of the sort of man who would eventually arrive at the front door and sweep me off my feet.

I was about twelve when Mum first showed me a picture of Ahmed. He didn't look like anything special, just one more face, so I didn't take much notice.

'Your grandma wants you to marry this one,' she said. 'He's a nephew of hers. She says it would be a good match for you both.'

I didn't say anything, still not believing that it was something I had to make a decision about yet, having heard it all before. I knew that by British law I had to stay at school for a few more years and I decided to worry about choosing the right potential husband when the time came. Mum must have put the photo away somewhere with the others because she didn't mention the matter again.

The following year one of the other girls in my class at school went back to Pakistan for a visit during the holidays. She came back for a while the next term, full of tales of how her family were planning to marry her off, which we all listened to open-mouthed, giggling behind our hands at the very thought of being married women, partly horrified and partly excited at the prospect of what lay in store for all of us. A few weeks later that girl disappeared. Her seat at school remained empty and no official explanation was given as to where she might have gone. Rumours began to circulate among her closest friends that she had been taken back to Pakistan and was now married to the man her family had chosen. I felt a tremor of unease at the thought that her family had been able to do that. If she could be made to marry at thirteen, might the same happen to me? I might not be interested in my schoolwork, but I certainly didn't feel ready to leave and become a married woman.

That same year we went on another family visit to Lahore because news had come through that Mum's father had died. Even though he had seemed so old I was sad to think I wouldn't see my grandfather again and I actually looked forward to going back out to Lahore to pay my respects and to see the other members of the family. I had enjoyed my other visits and often thought about them, and I was eager to show my grandmother how much I had grown up since the last time they had seen me. At the same time I was now nervous that they might have plans for me that they weren't talking about, just like the family of the girl who had disappeared from school. I told myself not to be so stupid, that Mum and Dad would never do such a thing to me.

Things had changed a lot when we arrived in Lahore,

partly thanks to the money that Mum and other members of the family had been sending home from abroad. My grandmother and her family had moved from the mud hut that they had been living in and had bought a house in the city, a solid building that was more like the sort of homes I was used to in Britain.

There were many things about life in Pakistan that I loved, such as the atmospheric calls to prayer that rang out across the city five times a day. They stirred all the deepest memories that I had stored up during the many, many hours I had spent in mosques as a child, pretending to be in prayer or reading the Qu'ran, soaking up the atmosphere without even knowing it. Although it had all seemed a bit like a chore in Britain, it had given me a sense of where I came from and of belonging to something bigger than myself. The calls from the minarets held an even deeper romance when I was actually in the land where the beliefs I had been given were so deeply rooted, the emotive voices sending shivers up my spine. As a child I might have grown impatient with the rituals and monotony of the religious observance my parents had insisted on, but it had still become part of my soul. Although part of me would never feel a hundred per cent Pakistani, I would always feel a hundred per cent Muslim.

There were other elements of street life in Lahore that I didn't like so much, like the way so many of the men would chew and spit in the streets and constantly seemed to be playing with themselves and hitching up their trousers as they stared aggressively at passing women. I felt threatened a lot of the time and wouldn't have wanted to walk around on my own out there in the way I always longed to do in Britain. Whenever any of us women went out in public we were always shrouded from head to foot, but I still felt vulnerable.

Ahmed, the relative whose picture Grandma had sent through to Mum, kept dropping in to the house for visits while we were there. He was only in his twenties, but to me he seemed like an old man, just another of the many uncles who I was always being introduced to without ever really understanding exactly who they were and how they were related to me. Whenever Ahmed was there the other girls would come looking for me, squealing with silly excitement.

'Guess who's here,' they would giggle, 'your future husband.'

'I'm not marrying him,' I protested feebly, pleased by the attention, but nervous in case it got out of hand. 'I'm not marrying anyone. We're just here for Grandad's funeral, not for anything else.'

'But Grandma wants you to marry him,' they told me gleefully. They obviously thought I had misunderstood the whole purpose of our visit.

I told myself that the idea was ridiculous, that I was still just a schoolgirl who lived thousands of miles away from all of these family concerns, but inside I felt a chill of apprehension. Was it possible that Mum and Dad were planning to marry me to this man the moment I was old enough? Had they made promises on my behalf already? It had happened to my classmate at school, and I had heard stories from other Asian families; might it be my turn next? I didn't have the courage to say anything to any of the grown-ups, I felt I had to bide my time and wait to be told what was planned before I could voice my protests.

Even though I had no intention of marrying him, I couldn't help but peek at Ahmed as discreetly as I could whenever he was there, wanting to see what sort of fate might have lain in store for me if I had agreed, wanting to see what sort of man it was that was showing an interest in me. He was a perfectly ordinary-looking, bearded man, certainly not drop-dead gorgeous, but not terrible either. He kept glancing at me whenever he walked past, shooting me flirtatious looks. I felt myself blushing whenever I caught his eye. As long as it didn't develop into anything serious I was rather flattered by his interest and started to return his looks for a few moments here and there, before quickly casting my eyes back down.

One of my cousins, who was married to one of Ahmed's

older brothers, got me on my own one day, her voice almost a whisper of conspiracy.

'Ahmed wants to talk to you,' she told me.

'Talk to me about what?' I wanted to know, not being able to imagine what I could possibly have to say to a grown man that would be of any interest to him.

'I don't know.' She looked flustered at having to explain something she must have thought was obviously not to be spoken about out loud. 'He just wants to talk to you. Come to my house and you can meet him.'

I didn't know how to refuse the invitation without offending her. It was also thrilling to be doing something so grown-up, but at the same time the chill of fear returned as if I instinctively knew I was moving into dangerous territory. My heart was thumping as I sat in my auntie's house later that day and by the time Ahmed finally came into the same room as me I could hardly breathe.

'What do you want to talk to me about?' I asked, trying to sound calm, hardly daring to look up from the floor.

'Do you like me?' he asked, getting straight to the point.

'No, I don't,' I said, preferring to run the risk of sounding rude to the risk of being accused of leading him on in any way. He opened his mouth to say something else, but the sound of other voices approaching the room obviously panicked him and he quickly left me on my own.

There must have been a lot of family gossip buzzing

back and forth around me, because by the time I got back to my grandmother's house later that day my brother Ali had heard that Ahmed had been alone in a room with me and had been flirting with me. Even though there were senior members of the family who wanted us to be married, Ahmed was still not allowed to be alone with me for fear that people would talk and I would be dishonoured. I was shocked by how angry Ali became at this infringement of his sister's honour. I thought he was going to hit me, but somehow he managed to hold himself back and stormed off instead to see Mum's younger brother, who was my favourite uncle, to tell him what he had heard about us. I had a horrible feeling that I had now provided them with the excuse they needed to marry me off quickly. By being alone in a room with Ahmed I had compromised myself and would not be able to protest at anything the men might propose. I felt sick with anxiety at the thought that I had played so completely into their hands.

'Tell this Ahmed that I want to speak to him,' Ali ordered our uncle with all the authority of a wronged man. My uncle had no choice but to do his bidding and Ahmed was duly summoned to my grandmother's house. When he arrived Ali greeted him coldly and insisted they went out together to the park for a serious man-to-man talk. Ahmed must have known he was in trouble, but he still went. It was as if they both had to act out this charade on my behalf.

Once Ali had him on his own he beat Ahmed up ferociously in order to show him just how valuable my reputation was and how badly they viewed his lack of respect for our family.

I was shocked when I heard what had happened and how violently Ahmed had been beaten. Although I was relieved that no agreement had been reached about us marrying, I felt even uneasier that my careless behaviour had led to this poor man being attacked on my behalf. I wondered if perhaps it was all my fault. Had I led him on by going to Auntie's house and by exchanging looks with him? The whole situation seemed so dangerous and grown-up and far from everything I understood, I didn't know what to say, and so I remained silent and hoped for the best.

Before we left the house to return to Britain, my grand-mother gave Mum a ring that she had been given by Ahmed's parents. Although there had been no official announcement or ceremony or even a proper introduction, it seemed that the elders on both sides had already decided that we should be considered as unofficially engaged, despite our mistake at Auntie's house and my brother's hot-headed response to it. I only found out about the ring when I overheard Mum telling Dad about it once we got home.

'Just put it back in the suitcase for now,' Dad told her. 'We'll see about it later, when the time's right.' I don't think he had any more idea of the plans Mum and Grandma had been hatching than I did. It's impossible to know how many of them were involved in planning my future at that stage without me knowing anything about it.

6
Falling in Love

Nothing more had been said about our visit to Lahore or about the engagement ring that still nestled in Mum's suitcase, awaiting its chance. It seemed I was not destined to be a child bride after all. I finished at school without knowing what was going to happen next. I was sixteen years old now and it had dawned on me that even though I had not done as well at school as some of my friends, staying in full-time education would be a way of buying myself a little more time before being married off and forced to live like the other women in my family. My exam results were good enough for me to be able to go on to sixth-form college if Dad would allow it. I thought that if I told him I wanted to do a business studies course I would be able to convince him that it would be good for the family because I would be able to get a better job and contribute more financially. I had no idea if Dad would allow it and I didn't dare to ask him outright, so I would drop hints to Mum and hope she was passing them on.

One day I decided to be brave and ask him outright.

'Dad,' I said, hardly daring to show him how nervous I was about asking the question. If he forbade it, I knew it would almost certainly mean he planned for me to marry immediately. 'I want to go to college, if you'll allow it. I want to become a businesswoman and earn lots of money. Please, Dad, let me go. My brothers go and they seem to be OK.'

I felt there was a glimmer of hope that he was willing to even discuss this. Maybe this was going to be a way for me to completely escape the fate that was befalling so many of the other Asian girls at school and my female cousins as their parents decided the time was right for them to give up education and marry. Once I had an education I might be more valuable to them unmarried than married.

'I will think about it,' he said, and I knew I had to be content with that. I left the room and Mum gave me a load of chores to do as usual. As I worked in the kitchen I could hear her trying to influence him in the other room.

'She's a girl,' she kept saying, 'girls don't go to college. There will be boys there. What will your brother and his family say?'

I kept praying that he would be strong enough to make his own mind up without listening to her. Finally he called me back into the room and asked me how much I wanted to go to college.

'It would be great if you would allow it,' I said, my eyes

humbly cast down. 'But if you decide against it that will be OK too.'

'I know I am going to get into trouble for this with your mother and with my family,' he said after a few more moments' thought. 'But I am going to give you a chance. Don't break my trust, Saira.'

I think that was the first time in sixteen years that I had smiled all the way from my heart, truly feeling happy. I had finally been given a chance to escape from my past and from the expectations of my family. I vowed to myself I would work harder than I had ever worked in school and would do nothing to let my father down now that he had finally shown faith in me.

My confidence was beginning to gather itself together by the time I got to college, but still hadn't risen nearly far enough for me to be able to act naturally with other students. Now that I was out of the all-girl environment of school I was forced to mix with boys all day long, having had no previous experience of talking to the opposite sex beyond my own brothers, neither of whom had ever been that nice to me. I had no idea what to say to boys or how to conduct myself in their company. I was constantly surprised when they were remotely pleasant to me, or even when they acknowledged that I existed at all. I wanted to be friendly and flirt with them, as I saw some of the other girls doing, but I was terrified of giving them the wrong message and bringing the wrath of my father and brothers down on my head and the heads of any boys who might be accused of dishonouring me when they would just have been being polite. It would have been mortifying to have had any of my college contemporaries invited out to the local park for a beating. My only hope of staying out of trouble was to keep my head down and my eyes on the ground and withdraw inside my own thoughts. I couldn't imagine how the other girls could be so open and confident around the boys and get away with it.

Although I was self-conscious around men and unsure how to act, it was also a relief not to be in an all-female environment, where everyone was competing with one another all the time, and where I felt most of the girls were looking down on people like me. I still had to be picked up from college by one of my parents or my brothers, which was embarrassing, but it was better than not being allowed to go at all.

'Is that your boyfriend?' the other girls would sometimes ask when they saw one or other of my handsome brothers waiting at the gates for me.

'No,' I would blush, 'it's my brother.'

'Why does your family watch you so closely?' they would ask, genuinely puzzled. 'Don't they trust you?'

I didn't have an answer to that because I didn't understand it myself. What had I ever done to make my family think that I couldn't be trusted to look after myself?

I found that I wanted to get to know the boys more than the girls. I liked their straightforwardness and good-heartedness. They didn't appear to be operating their own secret agendas, like some of the girls, but I had no idea how to start conversations with them, so I remained at a distance and alone most of the time.

As the weeks went by and my brothers seemed to be slackening their watch over me, my confidence rose a tiny bit higher and I started to look up from the floor and study the boys more carefully when they weren't looking. There was one in particular who I thought was really gorgeous and I kept watching him across the room, always averting my eyes as soon as he looked back, wanting to attract his attention and encourage him to come over and talk to me, but at the same time terrified of it, having no idea what I would say to him if he did. Simply daring to glance at him felt like the most incredibly brave thing to do. After a few days I knew he had noticed I was looking at him and he was even looking back towards me. I began to concoct all sorts of fantasies about how we would start talking and end up falling in love and I would actually get to choose the man I wanted to marry without any interference from my brothers, my parents, my grandparents or my aunts and uncles. I woke up every morning excited at the prospect of going into college and seeing him. My heart would start to thump whenever I was in the same room as him. When he made it clear through one of the other girls that he wasn't the least bit interested in me and didn't even want to talk to me, I felt crushed and humiliated.

I immediately sank down to my previous levels of self-loathing. How could I have been so vain and stupid as to think that such a gorgeous man would be interested in me? All my old insecurities about my weight and my skin colour and my lack of any sophistication came flooding back. I felt like the same tubby, smelly little girl I had been at school. Despite my burning humiliation there was nothing to do but keep going to college and to avoid looking at him at all costs, which meant I could hardly ever lift my eyes off the ground in case they accidentally met his.

There were a couple of other girls in the class I had noticed, who were both swathed in headscarves like me, but had much prettier and better-fitting clothes. After several attempts I managed to make some progress and become friendly enough with them so that I wouldn't be left sitting on my own all the time, looking like a complete loser. They were very kind to me, although it always seemed to me that they were really a team of two with me tagging along behind. By hanging out with them I slowly started to integrate with some of the other boys in the class and learned how to act more naturally around them, albeit in a painfully shy and modest way.

My brothers had both finished school by this stage and were trying to make their way in the adult world. Ali, the eldest, had always been ambitious and keen to prove himself. He was constantly trying to get in with the people whom he believed were making money, some of whom did not appear to me to be good or hard-working people. Despite the dubious company he was keeping, he still behaved like a dutiful Muslim man, working every hour possible in a takeaway food shop, saying his prayers and saving his money for the day when he would get married.

Another family from Pakistan who had been visiting us a lot brought a picture of their daughter and asked Mum and Dad if Ali would be interested in marrying her. Somehow an arranged marriage didn't seem as threatening to a man as it was to a woman. If it all went wrong he could always take another wife or just stay out of the home with his friends, choices that weren't open to a woman who made a bad marriage. There was also the fact that a man like Ali would have the necessary physical strength to make a woman do whatever he demanded.

He must have looked like a good prospect to the girl's parents. As far as they were concerned he had a steady job in the takeaway shop and seemed a good-looking and personable young man. They knew nothing of the people he liked to hang out with and whom he seemed to admire and want to emulate, nor did they know about his temper or his willingness to use violence when someone or something offended his high standards of behaviour.

Mum and Dad told the other family that they would like to open discussions about a possible match. They duly met the girl and liked her and things suddenly moved really fast, throwing the whole family into a whirl of activity and arrangements. Nothing cheers a family up as much as the prospect of a celebration like a wedding. Everyone became excited and happy and full of hope, even Mum, who was normally so weighed down by the worries and annoyances of the world. Having seen my photograph, the bride's family suggested that I would make a good wife for her younger brother, whose name was Aman, and everyone became even more excited. It was as if there was a marriage fever gripping the house and I confess I was a little swept up in it, wanting to be part of it, wanting to be the centre of attention like my brother and his bride-to-be.

There is something incurably optimistic in the hearts and minds of the young. Whenever someone suggested they were going to match me up with a boy whom I hadn't met and hadn't seen a picture of, I immediately imagined that he would be the nicest, kindest and handsomest young man I had ever come across, a true knight in shining armour. Ridiculously, I felt the same flutters of excitement in my stomach at the prospect that I was about to be paired up with this unknown brother-in-law. On that slim ribbon of romantic optimism, and against all the evidence of my experience so far, I began to picture myself being with him for the rest of my life, happily bearing and bringing up his children. The confidence that had been knocked out of me by the rejection I'd received from the boy at college reignited in my heart and I was sure that I now knew what the appropriate way to behave would be. I would not have to worry about what I should say to this boy because I wouldn't be allowed to talk to him until after the marriage anyway, and I knew the rules about being alone with him or allowing him to flirt with me. To my illogical young mind it seemed completely possible that my life was about to change for the better. If Ali could find a bride so easily, I reasoned, why should the same process not work for me? I liked my prospective sister-in-law, so why would I not like her brother just as much?

My photograph was taken to show to Aman and I waited to be told when a meeting had been arranged and we would get to at least see one another, even if we weren't yet allowed to talk.

Several agonisingly long weeks later the answer came back and Mum told me the result as we made breakfast together for Dad and my brothers. Aman, she said, had sent a message that he had no wish to meet me. His answer to the suggestion that we might make a good couple was an emphatic 'No'. Even though I had previously harboured no urgent wish to be married and had never met the boy, I felt as if I had been physically punched in the stomach as I listened to the words that Mum passed on with her usual lack of thought for my feelings. It seemed as if she was saying she would have expected as much, given how fat and ugly I was. But it wasn't her I felt angry with; it was this unknown young man. Surely he should at least have been interested enough to want to meet me before dismissing me out of hand? Was the photograph of me so hideous that he couldn't bear the thought of even setting eyes on me? All the hurt that I had felt after the rejection at college welled back up inside me and I had to look away so Mum wouldn't see the tears rising.

I set off to college that day with a heavy heart, lost in my own thoughts, grateful for once that the others all left me alone. Was I so unattractive that no decent-looking boy was ever going to be interested? Was it inevitable that I would have to marry someone old or ugly if I didn't want to die a spinster? As the day dragged past my thoughts began to crystallise a little, and the hurt hardened into anger. There was no point in being offended, I told myself, because he wasn't rejecting me personally since he hadn't even met me. So, how dare he make such a quick judgement just from being shown a single photograph? How did he know that I wasn't the one woman in the world for him if he didn't even take the trouble to meet me?

The questions kept swirling around in my head and I wasn't able to concentrate on anything in my classes as I fumed at the injustice and arrogance of his response. I felt as if this was far more disrespectful towards me than anything Ahmed had done in Lahore, but I knew the men in my family would not be coming forward to defend my honour this time, and Mum would just see it as confirmation that she had been right all the time about my lack of attractiveness. That night when I got home I didn't talk to anyone, still deep inside my own head as we made the evening meal and Mum babbled on with her many complaints of the day. No one noticed there was anything wrong, or if they did they didn't bother to say anything. Sometimes it felt as if I was completely invisible in the world. I continued to brood over the following weeks, and when the day of my brother's engagement party came I saw Aman for the first time, across a room crowded out with jabbering relatives.

That should have been the moment when I realised what a narrow escape I had had, but it wasn't. The man who had turned me down was the handsomest I had ever seen. I was shocked by how much I felt drawn to him, although he didn't even glance in my direction. I think he had forgotten all about being shown the photograph at that stage. It had obviously been a matter of no interest or importance to him, yet it had been eating into my soul for weeks. Even if he had looked across at me, I doubt if he would have connected me to the picture. I was just one more young woman in a crowd of them, my head down and my hair covered, my face bare of make-up. This glimpse of him, coupled with the lingering sting of his rejection, made the idea of being able to marry him now seem a hundred times more real and attractive. I practically felt like I had been jilted at the altar. Knowing that it would be completely inappropriate to talk to him directly, I casually asked the other women in his family to tell me about him and about the place where he worked. Not suspecting that I had any ulterior motives in asking, or perhaps already knowing that I had been turned down and taking a perverse pleasure in my futile interest, the women happily divulged everything they knew about him. He was obviously popular in the family and I memorised the name of the restaurant where they said he worked.

That night I couldn't get his face out of my mind, and I knew from experience how easy it was for me to allow a blow to my self-esteem to set me back for months or even years. Lying in bed, wide awake and brooding ferociously, I decided I wouldn't just accept this as my destiny. I would take my fate into my own hands and confront him, demanding an explanation for his decision to dismiss me as a candidate for his wife. I knew it was a dangerous path to follow, because he might well say something even more hurtful once he met me in person, particularly as he would be bound to see my approach as inappropriate behaviour for a young woman, but I knew it was a risk I had to take if I was going to shake off the black cloud of self-doubt that was hanging over me. After all I had nothing to lose and maybe everything to gain; nothing to lose as long as my brothers never found out, that was.

The following day after college, with every fibre of my body trying to make me change my mind, I walked to the restaurant where he worked and forced myself to go round to the kitchen door. I felt faint with nerves as I knocked timidly, half hoping that no one inside would hear me and I would be able to go home without executing my plan.

'I'm looking for Aman,' I announced when a young kitchen worker opened the door, wiping his hands on his apron and staring at me with a questioning expression.

'OK.' He nodded to another door which led through into the restaurant area before going back to his work at the sink, apparently no longer interested. He probably assumed I was one of Aman's sisters.

It was too late to turn back now so I mustered all my dignity and pressed on, moving quickly through the clatter and smells of the kitchen and into the calm of the carpeted restaurant. There were no customers and the men working there were eating a meal at one of the tables. One of them was him.

'Please can I speak to you, Aman?' I asked. 'My name is Saira.'

He stood up, looking surprised and embarrassed, still chewing on a mouthful of food. I glanced at him quickly before averting my eyes back to the carpet. He was just as gorgeous as I had thought at the party.

'I am Aman,' he said, as if I didn't know.

'Can we speak in private?' I asked.

'Sure.'

He ignored the sniggers of the other men and led me through to the bar area, indicating that I should sit down in one of the chairs where people sat for drinks or to wait for takeaways.

'Our families have been talking,' I said. 'They showed you my photograph.'

'I know,' he spoke kindly, not at all how I had imagined it would be, and I felt the wind of indignation that had carried me there going out of my sails. It wasn't as easy to be angry with him when he was so nice.

'I came to find out why you rejected me without even meeting me.'

'I . . .' he started to speak, but I was in full flow by then and just kept on babbling. 'How dare you make such a judgement just from a photograph? How dare you not at least do me the courtesy of meeting me and finding out what I was like as a person?'

He was glancing over his shoulder back towards his work colleagues, who must have been able to hear my raised voice.

'Would you like to go for a walk?' he asked.

'OK.'

I was nervous at the thought of being outside in the open with a man, but as I had come this far I thought I might as well keep going. I didn't think there was much chance of bumping into anyone who would recognise me in that part of town at that time of day. He held the door open for me and smiled so sweetly I had trouble even remembering how to put one foot in front of the other. Once we were walking I went back to haranguing him, partly to let out all my pent-up hurt and frustration and partly so I wouldn't sink into my usual tongue-tied silence. He stayed quiet and allowed me to talk myself dry. Then he apologised and it sounded like he really meant it.

'I'm so sorry,' he said. 'I think I was just scared that my family were rushing me into something I wasn't ready for. It wasn't personal to you. I would have said no to anyone they put forward. I shouldn't have done that. I should have given it a chance before making such a final decision. I should have considered your feelings, but you were only a photograph to me then, not a real person.'

He was so quietly spoken and gentle I felt that I had been shrill and unreasonable in the way I had attacked him. A little embarrassed by the way I had sounded off at him I allowed him to soothe my ruffled feathers as we strolled around the centre of town for a while and I became so lost in our conversation that I even forgot to be nervous about being spotted out, unchaperoned, with a man I was not related to.

'I have to get back to work now,' he said after a while. 'You go home and if you would like to meet up again, then let me know.'

As I headed back home I felt as light as air. All the hurt that I had been feeling, and the fear that perhaps I would never find a decent man who would be interested in me and that I would be forced to marry someone like my cousin in Lahore lifted away. He had actually been charming to me and he had said he would like to see me again. To my desperate ears that sounded as good as a full declaration of love, and all my fantasies about a big family wedding with a handsome groom by my side were reignited just as quickly as they had been extinguished by his initial rejection. That would prove to Mum once and for all that she was wrong about me being so unattractive, and would make Dad proud of his daughter for once. I felt so proud of myself for having found the courage to go to look for him and to confront him. I could hardly believe that I had done such a shocking thing, but now it seemed so easy and so obvious I could barely remember why it had taken me so long to pluck up the nerve in the first place.

When I got home I was bursting to talk about him and about how I was feeling. I wished I had someone I could tell about the whole adventure, but there was no one I could trust not to leak it back to my brothers or my father, and I could not get the picture of poor Ahmed being beaten up by Ali in Lahore out of my mind. The thought that Aman might get beaten up for talking to me when it had been all my fault was too terrible to even contemplate.

It didn't take me nearly as long to pluck up the courage to go back to the restaurant a second time a few days later, and again we went for a walk around the town centre together, chewing on baguettes, talking all the time as we tried to find out everything about one another. It was as if all my inhibitions had melted away, as if there was nothing I couldn't talk to him about. He was the first person I told about my dreams of being able to design textiles for a living, and he didn't laugh at my presumption as I assumed most men would. He seemed genuinely interested and asked me to bring some of my drawings to show him the next time we met. I couldn't work out if I was most excited by the fact that he wanted to see the designs or because he was suggesting he wanted to see me again.

I liked him even more than the first time and that feeling grew with every visit I paid to the restaurant over the coming weeks. The next time we went to a McDonald's for a burger, just like any normal modern couple going out together. Another day he booked himself off work and we took a bus to an out-of-town shopping centre. On another occasion we took a train to a completely different city. Apart from the family trips to Lahore, I had only ever travelled back and forth to schools and colleges. The sense of freedom and the infinite possibilities of a life away from my family felt intoxicating. For the first time ever I felt what it was like to be a grown-up, not a child.

As the date for the wedding between Ali and Aman's sister grew closer Mum and I spent more and more time visiting his family home. Often he was there when we arrived or he would come hurrying in while all the women were sitting around talking, and it was hard for me to keep myself from smiling and looking at him, which would have given the game away immediately to all the eagle eyes watching every move that the unmarried members of any family made. I'm sure other people must have guessed that we were flirting discreetly with one another at those gatherings, but they would never have imagined in a thousand years that we were meeting secretly almost every day, and for me that added to the excitement and romance of those weeks. Because of the way he looked at me and smiled I felt as if I was a beautiful swan emerging from the ugly duckling I felt I had been all through my childhood.

As the wedding day approached I spent more and more time fiddling with my appearance and, for the first time ever, Dad allowed me to buy some make-up. I hadn't a clue how to put it on, but my female cousins, who were all there for the wedding, got together to show me what to do. It was as if they saw me as some sort of project. Those were the happiest weeks I had ever known.

Aman and I had been seeing each other for about a month on the day that we decided to walk together to a park not far from the restaurant where he worked. We had bought some sandwiches and we sat on a bench to eat them, enjoying the sunshine, the fresh air and the scenery. Although I was self-conscious about being seen with a man in public, I still liked the idea that passers-by could see I was sitting with a boy. It made me feel that I was showing them I was just like them, not a member of some strange alien race, shrouded in scarves and living by different rules. As we finished eating he sat back with a contented sigh and I laid my head on his lap as if it was the most normal thing to do. I felt completely relaxed with him. I trusted him implicitly and just wanted to spend the rest of my life feeling like this.

'Close your eyes,' he said after a moment.

I did as he told me, savouring the feeling of being close to someone I cared so much about, feeling the breeze on my skin. I sensed him move but didn't open my eyes until his lips brushed mine and then he slid his tongue into my mouth. For a moment I was shocked and frightened, wondering what he was doing and how I should respond, but then I felt myself giving in to his kisses as if it was the most natural thing in the world. It was the most amazing sensation I had ever experienced. I had never felt so loved and so cared for. It was if I had been transported to another universe.

'How was that?' he asked after a moment, sitting back up, his fingers lightly stroking my cheek.

'It was OK,' I replied as nonchalantly as I could manage, unable to find words to describe how great it really was and how much I wanted to keep doing it. I can still remember the smell of his skin, even after all these years, and the longing I felt for him to hold me and press himself against me.

'Shall we do it again?' he asked.

'OK.'

We must have sat kissing on that bench for at least an hour before he finally had to get back to work and I needed to get home before anyone wondered where I was.

'Maybe we should get married,' he said as we wandered back slowly, both of us trying to put off for as long as possible the moment when we would have to part.

'Maybe we should,' I said, never having felt so sure about anything in my life.

Over the coming weeks we met whenever we could and whenever I was apart from him I could think of nothing else, longing to feel him against me again. Every chance we had to kiss and hold one another we would take, in a train carriage, in a back alley or a park, we couldn't keep our hands off one another, couldn't stop looking at one another.

We were holding hands one afternoon as we came back into the city centre, so drunk on love we didn't even think about who might see us, so happy that we had forgotten about the rest of the world, and forgotten also about who we were and where we came from. It was a few seconds before I realised that the man walking towards us was my brother Ali. The moment I realised I sprang away from Aman, but I knew it was too late and the sudden movement must have made me look doubly guilty. Ali was striding directly towards us. I could see Aman was worried too, but he was smiling, no doubt hoping that he would be able to charm his new brother-in-law out of his anger, making it seem like the most natural thing in the world that he and I should be walking together on our own. The next few seconds seemed to last forever and then Ali's slap landed on my cheek, sending me spinning from the force of his outrage. There were people all around, but Ali didn't care.

Everyone averted their eyes and walked round the unpleasant little scene, not wanting to become involved.

'Listen, Bro,' Aman said as Ali raised his hand to strike again, 'this is all my fault. Don't be angry with her.'

Ali's arm hovered for a second and then dropped back to his side. 'Get home now,' he ordered, 'both of you.'

Knowing we were in the wrong, but hoping we would be able to sort it out once we got home, we went with him. All the way there I wasn't able to stop myself from crying and shaking, partly from the shock of the slap and partly with fear of what everyone was going to say when Ali told them what he had seen. None of us spoke as we hurried through the last few alleys leading to the back of the house.

In the front room Mum was working at the sewing machine as always and Ali's new wife was sitting on the sofa, talking to her. They both looked up in surprise as Ali burst in, with us trailing behind like naughty school-children. They saw my tear-streaked face and must immediately have guessed what had happened, even before Ali started to punch Aman, knocking him to the floor. It was as if he was filled with an unnatural strength, fuelled by righteous anger and affronted honour. He didn't stop once Aman was down either, kicking and punching with all his might as we watched in a horrified silence. Aman didn't fight back. It was as if he accepted he was in the wrong and knew he had to take his punishment on my behalf. He curled himself into a ball and took the blows until eventually Ali came to a halt, panting from the exertion.

As Aman was physically thrown from the house my sister-in-law was left sobbing with the shame of her brother's transgressions, obviously imagining the worst, while I sat beside her, trembling with fear at what might be going to happen next. All we had done was have some time on our own together and exchanged some innocent kisses. Now it felt as if the whole thing had been a dirty, shameful affair, whereas before it had seemed like the most beautiful thing that had ever happened to me.

'I will never be going to your family's house again,' Ali roared at his wife as he stormed back in from ejecting Aman, 'and neither will you!'

Having done his duty, he strode out of the house to make some business call or other, leaving us both shaking and crying.

'What on earth has happened?' Mum wanted to know, finally getting up from the sewing machine where she had been rooted in shock by the sudden explosion of violence in her front room. 'What have you and Aman done, Saira, to anger Ali like that?'

'We just met a few times,' I said. 'I wanted to know why he had turned me down without even meeting me and we got talking. We really like each other.'

I should have expected her to react as violently as Ali,

but I was still taken by surprise by the ferocity of her punches as she threw herself at me, knocking me back against the wall, screaming abuse, telling me just how much shame and dishonour I had brought down on all our heads. She grabbed a shoe and was hitting me with it, over and over again.

'You have disgraced me and the family. How could you do this? I told your father not to let you go to college. I knew something like this would happen. You have shamed my womb. I have given birth to a lying, deceiving daughter.'

All the time she was hitting me with the shoe she was crying.

'I'm sorry, Mum,' I wept, cowering beneath the blows. 'Please forgive me. I won't do it again. Please don't tell Dad.'

Partly I was crying because I knew what would happen now that I had betrayed the trust Dad had put in me. I was petrified, but at the same time I still longed to be in Aman's arms and to feel him close to me. I knew he was the only person I could completely trust to stand up for me and protect me. I couldn't imagine how I would survive if I was forbidden from seeing him again.

7

My Wedding

By the time Dad came home from his shift at work that day I was still lying on my bed upstairs, sobbing, listening to Mum ranting and raving at her daughter-in-law downstairs as if it was all her fault, calling Aman and me every name she could think of. In my mind the happy weeks of the wedding had run on into my fantasy romance with Aman and now I had been brought back down to earth with a bang. Instead of being the romantic heroine I had been imagining myself to be I was back to being the object of everyone's derision and disgust. It seemed that my chances of a fairy-tale marriage were now in shreds and, according to Mum when she was at the height of her rage, I had made myself into some sort of soiled goods that no one was ever going to want. Worst of all I had proved her right and let Dad down when he had trusted me enough to allow me to go to college. I wished with all my heart that I could just be with Aman and he could kiss away all my problems, hold me in his arms and make everything all right.

I could hear Mum explaining everything to Dad

downstairs, but I couldn't hear his response. After a few minutes Mum shouted up the stairs, summoning me back down in order to confess my sins in person to my father, and I cried as I told him what I had done, expecting to receive yet another beating like the many I had received from him as a child. But a terrible calmness settled over him as he listened, almost as if he was giving in to despair and disappointment, as if he had finally relinquished any hope of forcing me to behave like a good Muslim girl, had finally accepted that I was only ever going to bring disgrace on the family. Now his wife and his brother and all his other relations would be able to tell him that he had been wrong to let me behave like a Western girl and this was the proof that they had been right all along.

I tried to explain how much I loved Aman, but I could see he wasn't interested in hearing any of what he would have considered my 'nonsense'. He seemed as concerned by what Ali's violent reaction would mean to our relationship with Aman's family as he was by what Aman and I might actually have done together.

'Very well,' he said when I had finished speaking. 'Leave it to me. I will sort it out. How does Aman feel about you?'

'I think he feels the same way I do,' I said, wondering if this was a glimmer of hope being held out to us. Was it possible that they would allow us to marry just in order to make the whole thing respectable? I hardly dared to hope. I didn't say anything because I knew that if that was decided they would want it to be seen as a punishment for my bad behaviour, not a reward.

'Let me phone him,' Dad said, obviously not yet willing to tell me what he was thinking.

He made the call and Aman came back to the house to see him, obviously nervous that he might receive another beating, but too respectful of my father to refuse his request. I loved him even more for being willing to face danger to protect what was left of my honour. When he walked into the house I just wanted to run over to him and throw my arms around him, clinging tight and never letting go, but I couldn't do anything like that. I had to stand all alone and listen to them talking as if I was no more than a problem to be solved.

'Is it true that you have been seeing my daughter in secret?' Dad asked him.

'Yes,' he said, bravely, 'it is true. I think very highly of her.'

'She says you have talked about marriage. Is that right?'

'Yes,' he said. 'But I need a little more time to get my thoughts straight. It has all happened so fast.'

I was shocked. This was very different to the way he had been talking to me when we had been alone. Now he was talking more like he was one of them, working out the best way to deal with a problem. Why did he need more time?

Surely he knew how he felt? That wasn't going to change, was it?

At that moment Mum came into the room. 'I'm sending Saira to Pakistan,' she told Aman, and my father said nothing.

'OK,' Aman nodded, apparently taking this new information in before turning to me. 'Go to your family for a bit of a break, away from Ali. When you come back our families can sit down and talk about what to do next.'

I felt that I could breathe again. He and Dad and Mum were just trying to find a way to calm the situation down, I told myself. They were allowing the dust to settle so that we could then announce our engagement in the traditional way and Ali would not lose any face. Although I didn't like the thought of being taken so far from Aman, I relaxed, believing again that things were going to work out all right in the end. Perhaps we hadn't ruined everything with our carelessness after all. I was being given another chance at happiness, I simply had to be a little patient. It wasn't too much to ask, was it?

It was arranged for me to travel to Lahore with one of my aunties and Mum said she would fly out to join us a few days later. I was worried that news of my disgrace would have travelled ahead of us on the grapevine and that I would be shunned by everyone as a punishment for having let down the family, but when we arrived at

Grandma's house everything seemed to be fine. I couldn't work out if that was because they hadn't been told of my disgrace or if they thought it was all going to be all right because Aman and I would be getting married as soon as I got back. Despite missing Aman, it was nice to see everyone again, and I decided to treat the next few weeks as a holiday.

Mum arrived a couple of weeks later and it was then that I started picking up things that other relatives were saying which made me uneasy once again. One day, for instance, I heard my cousins talking about having to have some new clothes made.

'What new clothes are you having made?' I asked innocently.

'Don't you know?' they said, suddenly looking embarrassed. 'It's for your wedding.'

'Don't be stupid,' I scoffed, trying to ignore the knot of fear that had suddenly tightened in my stomach. 'I'm not here to get married.'

'Yes, you are,' they said, as if it was a perfectly well-known fact.

I tried to dismiss the idea in my mind as ridiculous, but then I noticed that more and more relatives were turning up at the house as the days went by, and everyone seemed to be bustling about making preparations for some sort of celebration, putting up lights and decorations, but still no one had said anything to me officially. It was as if they were all avoiding getting into any sort of conversation with me. I eventually managed to get Mum on her own.

'What's going on?' I asked.

'It's your Mehndi tonight,' she said.

I had been to enough family weddings by then to know that a Mehndi was the night when a bride had the henna designs painted on to the backs of her hands, preparing her for her wedding ceremony.

'Aman is coming out here?' I asked, shocked that I should be the last to know but excited by the idea at the same time.

'Aman isn't invited,' she said, avoiding my eyes.

'Mum,' I said, desperately trying to keep my voice steady, 'I'm not getting married to anyone out here. I'm going to be marrying Aman when we get back to Britain.'

'He sent me a message before I left,' she said, still avoiding my eyes as she talked. 'He says he doesn't want to marry you. He was only playing about. He's thought about it and that is his decision.'

'He can't have said that.' I could hear her words, but I didn't want to believe them because I feared my heart would break if I did.

She shrugged. 'That is what he has said. If you don't believe me, phone your father and ask him. So you are going to marry Ahmed to save your reputation and to restore honour to the family.'

All I wanted to do was to talk to Aman and ask him why he would say such a thing, but there was no way anyone was going to allow me to do that now that the preparations for my marriage to another man were under way. There was no phone in the house and the only way to contact England would have been to go down to one of the local shopping malls and book a call through a local exchange. I would then have had to make the call in public with no privacy at all. I had no money and I wouldn't be allowed out of the house on my own anyway, so there was nothing I could do. I felt desolate and panic-stricken that my life was running out of control and that I could do nothing to stop it from heading down the wrong tracks once and for all. I wanted to run back to Aman as fast as possible, but I didn't have my passport because it was being looked after by my uncle, and I had no money for a ticket anyway. I might have been seventeen years old but I was as helpless as a small child. I felt as if my insides had been ripped out and my entire life had been trampled on.

One moment I had imagined I was going to marry the man I was madly in love with, the next I was being told he didn't love me at all and that I was going to marry a man I cared nothing for. It was all happening too fast for me to be able to do anything to stop it. There were so many people involved, all of them expecting me to behave like an excited young bride, none of them willing to imagine that my heart was breaking at the greatest betrayal I had suffered yet.

'Whatever happens I'm not marrying Ahmed,' I said, with no idea how I could actually avoid it now.

Mum opened her mouth to shout at me, but then obviously thought better of it and walked away. She had no need to fight me because she knew she had already won. In my innocence I took her silence to mean that she was accepting my decision and I thought that would be the end of the matter, but that night as I sat in the courtyard outside the house my favourite uncle came to sit with me. He chatted about nothing in particular for a while before coming to the point.

'Your mother and your grandmother are very upset,' he said. 'They really want you to marry Ahmed.'

I opened my mouth to protest but he raised his hand to quieten me.

'I know that you like someone else, but it's not going to happen. If you respect us like a good Muslim girl should respect her family, then you must trust our judgement in this matter. You have been promised to a decent, religious man from a good family. You have to go through with the marriage or else your father will never forgive your mother for arranging it. If you refuse now your mother will never be able to hold her head up in front of her family again. If you don't go through with this marriage you may never be able to go back to Britain again.'

He just kept on talking in his quiet, insistent voice, stressing the importance to the family of the match, and the importance of being dutiful and obedient to the elders in my own family, laying one layer of emotional blackmail on top of another. He never threatened me or shouted at me like Mum did, and as I listened to him in the hot evening air, aware that every other family member was watching us talking from their positions around the courtyard, I found myself nodding and agreeing with him and eventually giving in completely. It was my duty, I saw that now. And if I couldn't be with Aman then I didn't care what happened to me, I might just as well do the right thing by my family. If they all said Ahmed was a good man, then maybe he was. Having a good husband would be better than having no husband at all and maybe I would learn to love him a little as the years passed. The thought of never being able to go back to Britain again was the most frightening of all. Reaching the decision did nothing to lift the crushing weight that now lay on my heart, but at least it meant that everyone else could return to celebrating a wedding and enjoying themselves for a few days and I felt that I was making up for the shame I had brought on all of us with my careless behaviour.

Usually a family wedding like that would go on for weeks, but mine only lasted three days. I suppose they wanted to get it over with quickly in case I changed my mind about cooperating and started making a fuss. Perhaps they all knew that I had shown a dangerous spark of rebellion in Britain and believed that I needed to be brought under control as soon as possible in case I brought more shame on to all our families.

On the first night I had my henna ceremony. The following morning I was all dressed up in my wedding gown and Ahmed came to the house with his family. We were married by the priest in the courtyard of the house, which had been prettily decorated for the occasion. I should have been asked to recite some vows before signing the official piece of paper, but the priest didn't bother with any of the niceties, just thrusting the contract and a pen into my hand to sign with. Perhaps he too had been told that I was a disgrace to the family and had to be married off in a hurry in case I started making a scene. It didn't seem like a proper marriage to me but there were so many people involved now I didn't have the strength to protest and I didn't want to bring any more shame down on the family.

It should have been the happiest moment of my life but compared to the feelings I had experienced when Aman was kissing me and holding me it felt empty and false. I feared it marked the start of an interminable life of drudgery as the wife of a man I felt nothing for. It seemed as if I was set on exactly the same path of servitude and bitterness that my mother had been down.

After the ceremony I was taken back to Ahmed's family home to meet more of his relatives who hadn't come to the ceremony. They were all very nice to me and seemed to welcome me into their home as if they really wanted me to be there. This, I was told, was the house where Ahmed and I would be living as a married couple for as long as we were together in Pakistan. We would have our own room, which had been specially prepared for us, and I was taken to see it, obviously expected to show my gratitude at such generosity. The room had two doors, one of which led into the courtyard where the rest of the family lived, while the other opened directly into the alleyway behind the house, so that we could come and go without having to pass by everyone else should we want to.

Mum had been busy and had provided everything she could to furnish the room comfortably for me, buying me a bed, which had been decorated specially for the wedding night with streamers and ribbons, a sofa, coffee table, wardrobe, fan, television and hi-fi. It was by far the best-furnished room in the whole house; no one else even had a proper mattress. I suppose I must have looked rich to them with all these material possessions, which in Britain would have been considered the bare minimum in every home.

When Mum had asked me if there was anything else I wanted for the room I had said I would like a fridge, but once I saw how poor the rest of the family was I changed my mind, aware that if I did have one the whole neighbourhood would soon be queuing up at my door to use it, which might well cause jealousy and conflict.

I was informed that Ahmed and I would be staying there for a few months after the wedding until it was time for me to go back to my family's home in Britain. Once I was back there, I would then be applying for a visa for Ahmed to join me and we would be living the rest of our lives between the two family homes. I had reached a stage where I was feeling so numb I just nodded and accepted whatever anyone told me.

After we had visited the in-laws and seen the room, the wedding party then returned to Grandma's house because the tradition was for us to have one more night apart. The following morning I got all dressed up again for another family party that had been set up on a nearby piece of wasteground. In the end there were two or three hundred guests eating and drinking with us, all of them celebrating this great event. I would imagine most of the women knew from personal experience that the chances of future happiness for me must be slight, and perhaps they were all determined to enjoy the optimism for as long as it lasted. When everyday life is hard a party of any sort brings a welcome release from reality and everyone wants it to last for as long as possible. I should have been enjoying being the centre of attention, but the whole thing felt false and embarrassing. At the same time I didn't want the festivities to end because I was dreading whatever might be coming next.

8

The Marriage Bed

Despite the fact that I was now a married woman, I still knew nothing about sex beyond the fact that we had been taught at school how to put a condom on a banana. We were not told anything about when and why we might need to do such a thing to a real boy, or what we should do with him once the condom was on. The entire subject was a scary great black hole of ignorance that I preferred not to think about at all, and I couldn't understand how so many of the other girls at school had managed to seem so confident and knowing about the whole business. Maybe some of them were bluffing, but there were certainly others who knew all about it.

Kissing Aman and being unkindly groped and pinched by my brothers was the furthest that my experience with sexual activity had gone. The kissing, of course, had been wonderful and made me want to go further, but my brothers' attentions had seemed like a bad omen of what else men might want to do to me if they were given any sort of permission. Either way I was pretty sure there was going to be more to it than anything I had so far experienced. Unable to get my head round the enormity of the subject I put it right out of my mind, hoping that maybe it wouldn't happen for a long time. Obviously, I understood nothing about the urgency of men's physical needs.

By the third day of the wedding I still hadn't had a chance to talk to Ahmed and knew nothing about him at all beyond the fact that he was now my husband. After the party we all stayed at Grandma's, but there were only two rooms in the house, so many of us had to sleep outside in the courtyard. A big four-poster bed with straw for a mattress was placed in one corner for me and there were about five other beds set up around mine for other people, including my new husband. The men had all gone out somewhere when tiredness finally overcame me and I succumbed to sleep on my four-poster. I didn't hear them get back and had no idea that Ahmed had ended up sleeping on a bed that stood across the bottom of mine. The first I knew about it was when someone pinched me on the foot, waking me up with a start. As soon as I gathered my thoughts I realised that it must be my husband attempting to show affection and attract my attention. I tried to brush him away to show him that I wanted to be left alone. But he kept doing the same thing, like an annoying little boy.

'Go away,' I hissed, not wanting to wake anyone else up and alert them to what was going on.

Eventually he got the message and I was able to fall back to sleep. The next day he kept looking at me and trying to strike up a conversation, but I didn't want any of it. I felt so far from home and so threatened by things that I couldn't understand, I just wanted to withdraw to some private place inside my head and wait for the whole nightmare to be over – as if that was going to be possible.

The arrangements continued to be made without anyone asking for my opinion or preference about anything and two days later we returned to his family as a married couple. I knew that this was going to be the night that something was supposed to happen between us, but I had no idea how it was going to be or what I was supposed to do about it. As we headed to our marital home in a taxi I had a fearful sense of impending doom. However silent and withdrawn I might be, I couldn't stop events from continuing to unravel around me.

When we arrived I pleaded exhaustion and went straight to our room while he paid his respects to his family. I wouldn't have known what to say to anyone else at that moment anyway. Not wanting to have to undress in front of him I quickly got into my nightclothes while he was outside and climbed into the bed, listening to the unfamiliar voices of the people who were now my family talking just beyond the door. After a few minutes he followed me in. This, it seemed was the start of our married life together and I hadn't a clue what he was going to say or do. I kept my eyes firmly on my hands as he chatted away, introducing himself properly and telling me a few things about himself. He told me that he worked as a butcher and that he would have to go back to his job the following day.

'I have bought some sweets for you,' he said, proffering a crumpled bag.

'No, thank you,' I mumbled.

'Would you like a drink?'

'No, thank you. I'm really tired, I just want to go to sleep.'

He nodded his understanding and went to climb into bed with me.

'Can you turn out the light?' I asked, feeling the panic rising. 'I really want to go to sleep.'

He did as I asked and in the blackness I felt the blanket moving as he slid closer to me. I was rigid with fear as his hand crept on to my hip, pulling me over towards him. I stayed as still as I possibly could, fighting the urge to push him away, knowing that there was nothing I could do because he was my husband and he was allowed to paw me around if he wanted. I had no idea what he expected of me and he said nothing as he clumsily hitched up my nightdress and tried to satisfy himself. It didn't feel like he had any more idea what to do than I did because he made all sorts of attempts to penetrate me, but none of them worked, and I stayed stubbornly uncooperative as he became increasingly frantic in his efforts to consummate our marriage. Eventually he must have realised he was showing up his own lack of experience because he gave up trying and we lay silently together in the bed, both of us waiting for sleep to release us from our embarrassment. All I could think of was Aman and how much I wished it were he who was beside me in bed, preparing to spend the rest of his life with me. I tried to focus on the fact that I would be going back to Britain in a few weeks and would then have a respite from this married state before my husband was able to obtain a visa and rejoin me.

The next day Ahmed was trying very hard to be nice to me and I smiled at him a lot in order to be polite, but I just wanted him to hurry up and go to work so I could be by myself. It was hard to be in the company of a virtual stranger in such a confined space when there were so many things I wanted to think about. His sisters brought us in some breakfast, barely suppressing their shared giggles, and once we had eaten and he had gone off to work all the women in the neighbourhood started coming round to take a look at the new bride in the village and gossip with my mother-in-law. I could think of nothing to say to them but tried to answer their questions as pleasantly as I could.

By the middle of the afternoon I was feeling worn out again from the effort of being polite to strangers and when the remaining women finally went back out into the courtyard to cook and gossip, I said I was going to have a rest and stay in the room for a while. Almost as soon as the door was closed behind them, the other door leading to the alleyway opened and Ahmed came back in.

He had a determined look on his face as he climbed on to the bed beside me, undid his trousers and renewed his efforts to have sex. I still didn't have the slightest idea how to help him achieve whatever it was he was after and so yet again his attempts ended in disappointment, as they did again that night and three or four nights after that. It didn't seem to matter how hard he tried, he just couldn't find a way to force himself inside me. He was becoming more and more frustrated and embarrassed while I was getting more and more bored and annoyed with the discomfort of his endless fumbled attempts, which became rougher with every new failure.

To make it all the more unpleasant he had come straight back from his job at the butcher's shop, and he hadn't even bothered to wash himself or change his clothes before launching himself at me. I made a note to myself on the first day that I would always have a clean set of clothes hanging up waiting for him so he could change out of his blood-stained ones the moment he came in through the door.

Ahmed was determined to master the marital skills and continued to try several times a day until, a week after the wedding, we finally managed to get it right one night. But the effort of it all left him drained; after one mighty groan of pleasure he lay like a corpse on the bed beside me. Panicking that he might be having a heart attack and everyone would blame me, I ran out into the courtyard and upstairs to find my auntie, the one who was married to Ahmed's older brother.

'I think Ahmed is dying,' I cried. 'We had sex and he moaned and now he's just lying there and I don't know what to do.'

'Don't worry, my dear,' she patted my hand gently. 'That is often how men appear after they have done it. It's normal. Take him a glass of water, he will soon recover.'

I returned to the room feeling like a foolish child. Sure enough he was fully recovered a few minutes later and an hour after that he was ready to start all over again. This, I discovered, was to be the new pattern of our lives. He would demand to have sex with me four or five times a night, and then he would slip home from his job a couple of times during the day as well, always using the outside door to our room so the rest of the family never even knew he had come home at all. He was always in a hurry when he came home from work and was never willing to wash himself, let alone change his clothes, however much I begged him. It was as if he wanted to show me that he was the boss and he wasn't the sort of man who was willing to be told what to do by a mere woman, even if she was his wife. He didn't care that I was dry as a bone every time he penetrated me and within a short time I was so sore from his violent thrusting that I could hardly walk. It didn't matter how much I protested, whenever he felt like it he would just pin me down to the bed and hitch my skirts up. Every time he finished I would then have to get up and go and wash myself, because for a woman not to wash herself after the act would make her unclean. It sometimes felt like I spent the whole night going in and out of the room, while Ahmed fell straight to sleep after each time, waking a few hours later wanting to start again.

'Please,' I would beg, 'can you calm down because you are hurting me now.'

He must have heard my pleading, but he showed no sign of it, continuing to have his way all the time. I could have gone to the other women in the house for advice but I didn't want to make a fool of myself again after thinking he'd had a heart attack. As it was they were already making remarks about the amount of noise I made in the nights, keeping them awake. I realised they had mistaken my cries of pain for moans of pleasure, but I said nothing, simply blushing and looking away. Even if I had plucked up the courage to talk to them I am pretty confident they would just have told me I should be grateful to have a husband who was interested in me and that I should do whatever he wanted like a dutiful wife. I wondered if all men were the same and all women had to endure what I was enduring. If so, it would explain why so many women were bitter and angry and unhappy like my mother.

One night the pain became so bad that I found the strength to push him off me in the middle of the act and sprang out of the bed.

'You're not listening to me!' I shouted tearfully in my broken Punjabi. 'You are hurting me.'

I don't know if I got the words wrong, or if he just thought it was funny that I should even consider answering back to my husband, but he simply laughed at my anguish. Climbing out of bed he came across to me and for a moment I thought he was going to take me in his arms and comfort me, but he grabbed the nightdress I was wearing and ripped it open down the front, pulling me back on to the bed.

The next morning when I was crouching over the toilet in the bathroom the pain was the worst it had ever been. I put my hand down to try to soothe it with water but when I lifted my hand up I saw bits of what looked like torn flesh from inside me. It seemed to me, knowing nothing as I did about sex or anything to do with it, that I was literally being ripped to pieces. I was in so much pain I couldn't even pull myself upright and I toppled on to the cold, hard, wet floor, sobbing uncontrollably, wanting Aman to come to my rescue and knowing such a dream was impossible. Even in that foul-smelling toilet I could remember how sweet he had smelled when I kissed him and I felt as if my heart was being torn from my chest.

I soon realised there was no point in begging Ahmed for mercy or trying to appeal to his better nature. That only seemed to turn him on even more, as if my vulnerability made me more attractive to him. There was no point in saying anything at all, so I stopped speaking to him, unable to find any words for the thoughts and feelings and fears that were flooding my mind. I stopped looking at him too, afraid that any eye contact would merely inflame his desires even further. I also stopped getting into the bed, curling up instead on the sofa, being as uncooperative as possible every time he made his demands. I hid the ripped nightdress at the bottom of the wardrobe, embarrassed at the thought that anyone else would know how he treated me. It wasn't long before everyone else in the house noticed that I wasn't speaking to him and his youngest sister was deputed to come and talk to me.

'Are you refusing to speak to my brother?' she asked as if this was somehow an insult to their whole family.

'Has he told you what he has done to me?' I replied, feeling all my repressed anger bubbling dangerously towards the surface.

'No.'

I got the impression she didn't want to hear any criticism of her brother from an outsider like me.

'Then, let's just leave it at that,' I said, not wanting to give away any more of my dignity than I had already lost.

Realising that I was not in a mood to be won round, she went back outside, probably to report our brief conversation to her mother and the other older women. I guess they talked about me among themselves for a while, and when my sister-in-law came back into the room an hour or two later her mood seemed to have darkened considerably. She announced she was looking for a scarf she had lent me. I suppose she was thinking she would punish me for my surliness by taking it back.

'It's in the wardrobe,' I said, without getting up from the sofa.

As she searched for the scarf she picked up the torn nightdress that I'd thrown in there. She held it up and examined it. When she turned to face me she was laughing mockingly.

'What happened here?' she teased.

'Your brother did that,' I said, 'but I don't find it as funny as you do.'

Shrugging, as if to say she had only been trying to be friendly, she scrunched it back into the bottom of the wardrobe and left with her scarf. Later that day my auntie was sent in to try talking to me.

'I hear you are not talking to your husband,' she said.

'Has he told you what he has done to me?' I asked again.

'What has he done?' she asked kindly, sitting down beside me and taking my hand in hers.

I explained how he wanted sex all the time and how he had damaged me inside by being so rough.

'Oh, don't worry,' she said. 'That's just because you're a newly-wed. You'll soon heal over. It's the same for all of us. His brother still wants to do it every night and we have been married for years. You get used to it.'

'I don't think I can, Auntie,' I said. 'It is so painful.'

'I tell you what you should do,' she said after a moment's thought. 'The two of you should go and stay with his sister for a few days. It will give you a break and a chance to get to know each other better, away from all of us and all the family pressures. It will be like a little honeymoon.'

I knew that Ahmed's sister lived in a village some way away and I thought perhaps she was right and it would be a good idea to get out of our one room and away from all the prying eyes and ears of the others. If we were staying in someone else's house he would probably leave me alone a bit more and my soreness would have a chance to heal. Ahmed agreed to the idea immediately, which made me wonder what he was up to, and arrangements were made for us to travel together the following day.

The trip to my sister-in-law's house took about seven hours in a hot, crowded public bus, and we stopped along the way a few times for rest breaks, buying food and drink from the usual stallholders who lined the roads with their wares. None of the stalls looked that clean, but the other passengers didn't seem bothered by the lack of hygiene and I was hungry and thirsty enough to be grateful for whatever I was given. A few hours into the journey, having eaten and drunk my fill and slept for a while, I woke to feel some uncomfortable stirrings in the pit of my stomach. A light sweat broke out through the pores of my skin.

'I think I have eaten something bad,' I whispered to Ahmed.

'You'll be all right,' he said, 'don't make such a fuss.'

I didn't share his confidence, but I could see there was no point in hoping for any sympathy, so I stayed quiet and hoped for the best as the bus crashed on and the light outside started to fade.

When we finally arrived at our destination I realised the village was a great deal poorer and more rural than any I had visited before, with no electricity at all. It was completely dark by then, apart from a slither of moonlight, and we had to walk through fields of mud from where the bus had deposited us, unable to see what we were treading in until too late, our stumbling progress accompanied by the sounds of an invisible orchestra of insects. The stirrings in my stomach were developing ominously and I was beginning to feel very unwell. I was afraid I was about to be sick or have an upset stomach or both as we kept on walking across open land for what seemed like an age until coming to the ragged settlement of buildings. When we reached a gate in the wall surrounding Ahmed's sister's house, he went in ahead of me to find her, and as I stepped through the wall into the courtyard I found my relatives already whispering furtively by the light of an oil lamp, their distorted shadows dancing around the walls. By that stage I was feeling too ill to care about anything apart from the waves of nausea that were threatening to overwhelm me.

'Can you tell me where your toilet is?' I asked before even saying hello.

'What do you want to do?' she asked. 'Number one or number two?'

'Why?' I asked, startled by such a personal question.

'Because if it is number one you can do it on the bathroom floor and wash it away down the drain. If it is number two you will have to go in the field.'

The thought of setting back out into the night across fields I didn't know was more than I could cope with. My sister-in-law could see how distressed I was becoming and took pity.

'I tell you what I will do,' she said. 'You sit here and I will get some sand in a bucket. You can do your business in that. Just cover it up till the morning.'

She brought me a drink as well and I immediately started vomiting into the bucket. It felt as if my body was trying to eject everything it contained and my temperature was rising as the fever took a hold. All the time this was going on Ahmed was still whispering urgently in his sister's ear, goading her to arrange something for him. I heard snatches of what he was saying and it sounded as if he wanted us to be given a room inside the house so that we didn't have to sleep in the courtyard with the rest of the family.

'It seems he can't bear to be apart from you for a moment,' she said when he was out of earshot.

I knew exactly why he was asking for this to happen. Even though I had told him how much intercourse was hurting me at the moment, and even though I was throwing up violently, he still wanted to have sex. Not feeling strong enough to even attempt to explain everything to his sister I went along with the plan and allowed her to lead me into a room and to help me lie down on the bed. When Ahmed came in I told him as firmly as I could, while I lay sweating between vomiting attacks, that there wasn't going to be any sex that night.

'Please,' he pleaded. 'I promise I'll only do it once. Then I'll let you sleep. Please.'

His sister came back in at that moment and he moved away to wait in the shadows on the other side of the room.

'I've brought you some tablets for the sickness,' she said, helping me to sit up enough to swallow them.

A few minutes later, when she had left us alone in the room again, I began to feel an overwhelming tiredness. I don't know whether it was the long day we had had, the sickness or the tablets she gave me, but my limbs felt so heavy I could hardly lift them. Maybe it was a combination of all these factors. I had placed the bucket next to the bed so I could just roll over and use it with minimum effort every time another wave of nausea rose to the surface. Ahmed lay down beside me and put his arm round my waist as if to comfort me. Half delirious with exhaustion and dehydration, I suddenly realised that he had climbed on top of me, ignoring everything else that was going on. Forcing his way inside me, he was soon pumping away again as usual. I tried to find the strength to push him off, but it was hopeless, there was nothing to do but wait for him to satisfy himself.

I passed into unconsciousness before he had finished and whenever I surfaced every few hours in order to throw up again I was only vaguely aware of what was going on. When I finally woke up in the morning I was so sore it felt as if he had been inside me all night. When his sister saw me in the light of day she could see that I was much more ill than she had first thought.

'You need to take her to the doctor,' she told Ahmed.

That meant taking a trip into the nearest town and I was still half out of it by the time we got to the consulting room. Ahmed explained that I was from Britain and the doctor told him to wait outside the room while he examined me. Once we were on our own he laid me out on a stretcher and took some blood. I was hardly conscious, but after a minute or two I realised that rather than examining me he was actually feeling my breasts for his own entertainment. When I protested he stopped and called Ahmed back in as if nothing had happened.

'I have taken some tests,' he explained. 'If you bring her to my house this evening I will be able to give you the results.'

The moment we were outside the surgery I told Ahmed I wanted to go back home. I certainly didn't want to have anything else to do with the doctor. I was beginning to wonder if every man in Pakistan was the same. Was that why young girls had to be guarded so ferociously by their families? Or was it the other way round? Was it because all the men were so starved of sex that they grabbed every opportunity they were given to grope and squeeze?

I had already noticed that it was impossible for women to walk anywhere in crowds without having their bottoms or breasts pinched by strangers, or without finding someone's fingers wriggling around between their legs. It seemed to happen to virtually all women apart from the very old. The female relatives I had talked to about it all seemed to accept it as normal and unavoidable; men, they seemed to be saying, would always be men and there was nothing we could do to change that.

I never thought when I was living in Britain with them that I would end up missing my overprotective brothers and parents. I felt that I couldn't trust anyone in the new world that I now inhabited. Ahmed refused to allow me to get out of the second appointment with the doctor, partly I think because he was worried about my health, but also because he was in awe of a man with a qualification and didn't feel it was his place to disobey the doctor's orders.

In the end I had to give in, being too weak to go anywhere on my own. 'But don't leave me alone in a room with him,' I pleaded. 'I want you there all the time.'

Once we were inside the doctor's house he asked Ahmed to leave the room again, but I summoned all my strength to demand that my husband stayed. Both men were obviously embarrassed by my outburst, but not surprised. Maybe they even thought my modesty did me credit, that this was how good Muslim women were supposed to behave. They had forced me to conform to every stereotype that I had hated when I was living in Britain. I had become a woman who believed all men were potential attackers and who felt in need of protection at all times from other members of her family.

The doctor told Ahmed that his tests showed I had malaria, which was why I was burning up. 'She is also pregnant,' he added.

I heard his words through the haze of sickness and pain, but said nothing. I hardly even felt anything. It just seemed like one more disaster on top of everything else. I vaguely wondered what would happen next. Would this mean that I would have to stay in Lahore until the baby was old enough to travel, or would I be able to go back to Britain to give birth? The thought of delivering it in a hospital in Lahore, or worse still in my mother-in-law's house, was terrifying.

'Is it true?' Ahmed asked as we left. 'Are you pregnant?'

'I don't know,' I murmured weakly. 'I've never been pregnant before, so I don't know what the signs are.'

If I was pregnant then it had certainly been a quick conception, but given the number of times he'd had sex with me in the previous weeks it wouldn't be surprising. Even though he had been told by a doctor that I had malaria and that I was carrying his baby, he still demanded to have sex again that night as soon as we got back to his sister's.

The next day, although I was still feeling weak, having not eaten for several days by then, I insisted that we got the bus back to our own home in Lahore, even though it meant travelling in the heat for seven hours. I wanted to talk to my uncle, the only person out there whom I believed truly had my best interests at heart. A few days later I was strong enough to make the journey to my grandmother's house and asked my uncle if I could talk to him alone.

'Please take me away from there, Uncle,' I said, unable to hold back the tears at the sight of a friendly face. 'I can't cope any more.'

'Soon you will be going back to Britain,' he said, trying to comfort me. 'Can you not stay with your husband just till then and honour his family?'

I couldn't bring myself to speak to him about all the personal reasons why I needed to get away, but he could see from my desperation that I was near to breaking down. 'Please, let me stay here with you,' I begged, 'just until it is time for me to fly back to Britain.'

'All right,' he said eventually. 'I'll explain to Ahmed.'

Once in the safety of Grandma's house I couldn't stop myself from crying. It was such a relief to be left alone to sleep at night and not to be receiving disapproving looks all the time. Uncle was very sweet to me, assuring me that I didn't have to go back to Ahmed until I felt ready. I thanked him, but in my heart I knew I would never be ready. Maybe he was able to guess what the problem was and thought that I simply needed some time to heal and gather my thoughts a bit.

Uncle was only about five years older than me and so it was natural that we would spend time together over the next few days. In some ways we were like friends. We went for burgers or juices and he would put me on the back of his motorbike to ride around Lahore. He even persuaded me one time to sit at the front and hold the handlebars, which was a great feeling, the wind whipping through my hair, allowing me to forget all my worries for a while and simply to enjoy being young and free. I didn't like going out on the motorbike so much at night because of the wild dogs that scavenged by the sides of the road. They would chase us, barking and snapping around the wheels and our ankles.

Moments like that made me all the more aware of just how much I had lost by getting married so young to a man I didn't even like very much. Because he was my uncle it was considered perfectly respectable for him to take me out now that I was a married woman. Uncles are seen as father figures in families like ours and not assumed to be a threat to their nieces' virtue in any way. We were having fun like any young people might do.

'Do you fancy going to the cinema?' he asked me one day.

Not having realised they even had one in the neighbourhood, I excitedly wrapped myself up in my scarves and we headed off into the busy evening streets. The outside of the building looked like nothing special, but as we shuffled and jostled our way further and further towards the centre of the action the pressure of the crowds built up. There were herds of people everywhere, all shouting and laughing. There were some seats in the auditorium, but most people stayed standing so they could see better what was going on, and so they could dance and sing more freely once the film started, all of them whistling and cheering the on-screen action. I had to go through into the small women's section. At moments like that I felt a mixture of excitement and amazement at the culture my family had come from. It all seemed so alien and overwhelming. The men were going wild with excitement, free from the inhibitions of being with their families or with women, and as I watched them shouting and dancing and embracing one another I felt like an onlooker from another planet.

Ahmed arrived at my grandmother's house two days later and said he had come to take me home. Uncle must have been able to see from the look of horror on my face that I didn't want to go and he said that I wasn't ready to return yet.

'Just leave her with us for a little longer to regain her strength,' he said, and Ahmed had no choice but to agree. It was obvious that he only wanted me back for one reason.

The next day Ahmed's father came and sat down with my uncle. 'This will be their first Eid together,' he said. 'So we would like Saira to be there with us and with her husband.'

Uncle came to find me and tell me. 'I'm sorry,' he said, 'I can't turn down a request like that, not from your father-in-law. Just go for a day or two and then I'll bring you here for the last few days before you fly back to Britain.'

When I arrived back to my marital home nothing had changed. Ahmed gave me some money so that I could buy some clothes and jewellery to wear during Eid, and my aunt said she would go down to the market with me. He had given me about twelve pounds in British money, but out there it was enough for me to be able to buy him a pair of shoes and a suit for myself and a few more little presents. I gave him the shoes when we got home, but he didn't like them. I suppose they were more the sort of thing that young men in Britain would wear than Pakistani men. It reminded me how far apart we were in virtually every way. I didn't understand him any more than he understood me.

'How much did you spend?' he asked.

'I don't know,' I said, suddenly flustered. 'I just spent the money that you gave me. I didn't memorise the prices.'

But he wanted to know exactly how much everything had cost and I realised I must never assume that he was just being generous when he gave me money to spend.

I wanted to make a contribution to the family festivities and asked my mother-in-law what I should do to help.

'Make something sweet,' she instructed. 'Sweet rice.'

Although I had always helped Mum in the kitchen I had never actually cooked something all on my own, but I didn't want to admit that to them for fear they would think I believed I was too good to work in the kitchens with them. I tried to remember everything I had seen Mum do but it was no good. The mixture I concocted stuck together like bread and had to be thrown away, which was a terrible waste in a family where money was in such short supply.

'Look what the stupid cow has done,' my mother-in-law announced to the whole courtyard. 'Didn't her parents teach her to cook anything?' I felt I had let Mum down yet again by not being a good daughter-in-law.

The next day I helped with the laundry, sitting on a tiny stool in the courtyard, scrubbing away with nothing but a cold tap and bar of soap. I could feel the eyes of all the women watching me, but none of them offered to show me the best way to perform the chore. They had decided now that I was a spoiled girl who needed to be put in my place and taught a lesson, so that I would learn to be a better wife and daughter-in-law. I remembered how they had all reassured my mother before she flew back to Britain. 'Don't worry,' they had cooed into her ear when it had looked like she might cry, 'Saira is our daughter now too. We will look after her like she was our own.'

9

The Visa

Finally the day came when I was due to fly back to Britain. It felt like the end of a prison sentence. Even though I knew it would only be a matter of time before I had to be reunited with my husband, it still felt as if I was being set free. Once we were living in Britain, I reasoned, we would be on my home territory rather than his and he wouldn't be able to make so many demands without his whole family there to back him up. I wouldn't be as isolated and vulnerable as Mum had been when she married Dad. Although I didn't get on well with my brothers, I knew that they would take a terrible revenge on anyone who disrespected me, and Ahmed knew that too, which would give me at least some bargaining power in the relationship.

The streets of my home city looked so clean and comfortable as we drove in from the airport, with passers-by all wearing shoes and decent clothes and all going about their business rather than hanging around on the streets staring at people. When I was out in the town centre the next day it felt so good to be able to actually walk through a crowd on my own without being constantly jostled and groped by strange men. At home I could take hot showers and baths whenever I felt like it, or help myself to food from the fridge. I promised myself I would never take these little luxuries for granted again. Best of all when I went to bed I could feel safe that I wouldn't be woken up or molested while I slept.

I was eighteen now and eager to earn some money to help Mum and Dad with all their growing financial problems. I quickly found myself a job in a sandwich shop and set about filling in the necessary forms for Ahmed to be given a visa to follow me. Personally I was in no hurry to see him again, but my family knew where their duty lay and so they kept nagging me to get the job done, checking that I wasn't putting it off. I think they liked the idea of having another potential breadwinner in the country more than the prospect of having another unattached woman to look after. Mum probably liked the idea of having another member of her family around as well, after years of being outnumbered by Dad's relatives. In fact from the moment I started work in the sandwich shop I was bringing more money into the family than Mum or either of my brothers since all three of them seemed to have run up debts that were soaking up every penny they made in interest payments. I could see that my parents were worried about the way their sons' lives were going, but none of us liked to challenge Ali or Asif because their tempers were so violent if anyone questioned them. Now that Dad was getting older, and both boys were infinitely stronger and more violent than he had ever been, even he seemed to prefer a quiet life and didn't question them about their lifestyles.

I tried to explain to Mum and Dad that my marriage to Ahmed hadn't worked out and that I would like to divorce him, but they wouldn't even listen to such talk. Mum ranted and raved about how I was trying to bring yet more disgrace to the family and Dad advised me that I must be patient and give it time, assuring me that marriage was difficult for everyone in the beginning. I dare say in many ways he was right. I don't think marriage was easy for him with either of his wives, and it certainly hadn't been easy for the two women either, but I didn't believe that meant I had to accept the same fate. The marriage to Ahmed had been of their making, not mine, so why should I not be allowed to say it was a mistake, just as Dad had done with his first marriage? I might have been having all these thoughts in private, but I still wasn't nearly brave enough to speak them out loud. I was very aware of how badly I had shamed the family with my behaviour so far and I knew that I had to make it up to them in any way they chose. I was also enjoying the feeling of being away from Ahmed and didn't want to spoil it with unnecessary family rows.

As soon as I got home I made an appointment with our doctor, who confirmed that I was pregnant. I think I had been clinging to the hope that the first doctor had been mistaken as it was so early in the pregnancy, and hearing it confirmed so definitely felt like a death sentence. I knew from the expression on Ahmed's face when the first doctor told him the news that he believed this baby would guarantee his chances of being given a visa. If he had a wife and a child in Britain, who could deny him entry? I also knew that if I had a child it would be a hundred times more difficult than ever to persuade my family to allow me to divorce Ahmed and it would make it much harder for me to earn the money that I needed in order to help Mum and Dad.

Two days later, however, I suffered some heavy bleeding and miscarried the baby in the night. First there were the agonising pains and then the blood, and then a terrible, exhausted sadness descended on me. Although it was an enormous relief in one way, I was sad too to think there was no longer a little life beating away inside me. Ali's wife had a lovely little boy, Sulaiman, who was the sweetest little thing I had ever seen. I would have loved to have had a child like him of my own, especially if I could have had it with Aman, but there was no way I wanted to have Ahmed's baby, and I would never be able to forget the pain that he had put me through during the time the child was conceived. To overcome my sense of loss I would spend hours playing with Sulaiman, who was just over a year old and starting to walk and talk, always volunteering to babysit him if I was at home. There were moments when it felt as if I had bonded with him so firmly he was actually my own child.

One of the things I wanted to do more than anything else when I got back was to talk to Aman and find out why he had changed his mind about marrying me so completely. But when I plucked up the courage to ring him I found that his number had been changed and no one else in the family would tell me how to contact him. It was as if someone had given orders that we were to be kept apart at all costs. I was so furious with him that there were times when I thought perhaps I would make a real effort with my marriage to Ahmed just to show Aman that he wasn't the only man in the world who loved me, that I was perfectly capable of finding a good husband and that I didn't need him in order to find happiness and fulfilment. In reality, of course, I was still deeply in love with him and knew that Ahmed wasn't half the man Aman was, whatever way you measured them.

Once we had filled in all his visa application forms in Britain, Ahmed had to travel to the British embassy in Pakistan to be interviewed. He was provided with a translator since he spoke no English. My father and brothers offered to help coach him down the phone in the sort of questions he would be asked, but he brushed their offers aside.

'I will just tell the truth,' he scoffed arrogantly. 'I know what I am doing.'

Obviously he didn't.

'What was your primary purpose for marrying?' his interrogator at the embassy enquired.

'To gain entry to the United Kingdom,' he replied.

I dare say that was the honest answer, but it certainly wasn't a wise one to give, unless he was deliberately trying to sabotage his chances of getting into Britain for some reason no one else knew about.

Startled by such honesty, the embassy official assumed there must have been a misunderstanding in the translation.

'Do you completely understand the question?' he asked.

'Oh yes.' Ahmed nodded enthusiastically, no doubt eager to show how intelligent he was.

'So, I will ask again, what was your primary purpose for marrying?'

'To gain entry to the United Kingdom.'

With that proud, truthful statement he closed off any hope he might ever have had of being given a visa to live and work in Britain, the land of opportunity for so many men like him. I would imagine the officials decided at that moment that they weren't going to grant him a visa, but they kept asking the required questions anyway, going through the motions.

'What does your wife do?'

'She is a seamstress.'

They already knew that that wasn't what I did, and every answer he gave after that showed that he didn't know me or my family at all.

'What does her father do?'

'He is a taxi driver.'

'What is your wife's date of birth?'

'I don't know.'

When I heard that his request for a visa had been turned down I felt that perhaps there was a glimmer of hope for me after all. Maybe my parents would relent and allow me to divorce him now they could see that he was too stupid even to get through an interview. I said nothing, not wanting to insult them by suggesting they had made a bad choice of husband for me, and waited to see what would happen next.

After being back in Britain for several weeks I finally managed to track down Aman's telephone number through a mutual friend who knew nothing of the history between our two families. Shaking with nerves I dialled it, my heart jumping when I heard him answer.

'Where are all your promises now?' I asked, without even introducing myself. 'You said you wanted to marry me and then you turned round and said you had never meant it.'

'I never said that,' he protested, sounding genuinely shocked by the accusation. 'I was waiting for you to come back to Britain like you promised. Who told you I said that?'

'My mother.'

Something in the tone of his voice suggested that he might be telling the truth.

'They told me you were marrying someone else in Pakistan,' he said quietly. 'It broke my heart. I believed you had gone away for a holiday and then I heard you had got married.'

He explained that believing I had betrayed him, he had done the same as me, and allowed his family to arrange another marriage to someone they deemed to be more suitable for him. It had been a plot hatched behind our backs between our families, and we had both been duped, all because we had gone out for a few walks together in the city and brought some perceived disgrace down on them all. We had never even been alone in a room together, and no one knew that we had kissed so fervently. I couldn't believe what I was hearing. I had been tricked into losing the man who I was now sure was the love of my life, and there would never be any hope of undoing the damage that had been done as a result.

'You are engaged?' I felt as if I had been punched in the stomach.

'Yes.' I could tell from the tremble in his voice that he was as devastated by what had happened as I was. 'You will be invited to the wedding.'

The idea of it was too horrible to contemplate, but I knew that I would have to attend if I didn't want the whole world to know that my heart was broken and that I was married to the wrong person. The following few weeks were the most agonising time of my life. At one point during the wedding ceremonies I actually had to leave the room for fear that I would break down in front of everyone. There are family videos where you can clearly see me running out, but nobody has ever commented. The festivities went on for days as usual and all the time I had to keep up a cheery façade, making polite conversation with relatives I hardly knew, never sure which ones had or hadn't heard on the family grapevine about how Aman and I had disgraced ourselves before being forced to marry other people. Every time I saw someone looking at me I felt sure they could see into my heart and knew that it was breaking under the weight of my sorrow, and all I could think was that they would be whispering to one another that I had brought it on myself, that I deserved the fate that had befallen me because I had let both our families down.

His wife was very nice, so even if I had wanted to hate

her for taking the love of my life I wouldn't have been able to. She was much more beautiful than me, but then I always thought every other woman was more beautiful than me because that was what my mother had been telling me all my life.

Once Aman was safely married I was able to talk to him more openly at the family parties with less fear of causing a new scandal and I told him how devastated I had felt during the wedding festivities.

'How do you think I felt when I heard that you were getting married in Pakistan?' he asked.

'At least you didn't have to actually watch it,' I snapped.

'I could imagine it,' he said quietly, 'and perhaps that was even worse.'

We didn't see each other for a while after that and I tried very hard to put him out of my mind, but however hard I tried my thoughts kept coming back to him. It must have been the same for him because about six months after his wedding he phoned me again.

'Our new house is being decorated,' he said after a few minutes of polite and stilted conversation. 'Would you like to come and see it?'

I don't know if he actually wanted to show me his home, or if he planned for us to go to bed together from the moment he decided to ring, but that is what happened. In the empty house, among the dust sheets and stepladders, we uncovered his marital bed, which was virtually the only piece of furniture in the house, and made love just as I had been fantasising ever since I first set eyes on him. Because we had both had experience of the marriage bed by then we knew better what we were doing and there was none of the awkward fumbling that there might have been if we had been each other's first lovers.

'My husband has been very rough with me,' I told him as he took me in his arms. 'He's hurt me and sex frightens me.'

'This won't be anything like that,' he assured me, and he was right. 'Just say if it hurts and I will stop immediately.'

It didn't hurt because he did it perfectly and his skin smelled and felt just as wonderful as I remembered. After we had finished he lay with me in his arms, gently stroking me. If I had believed I was married to the wrong man before, I was even more certain by the time I left the house that day. The happiness I felt at having made love with the man I loved was completely overshadowed by my sadness at the thought of what I had lost, and by my guilt at the sins we had both just committed in that empty house. There was no doubt about it now, I had truly let down my family with my behaviour and if they ever found out the retribution would be too terrible to contemplate.

We met a couple of times more at the house when his wife was at her mother's, neither of us strong enough to

resist the temptation, but we both knew it was too dangerous for us to continue for long. If we were caught there
was a very real risk that the men in my family or in his
wife's family would kill both of us. They would certainly
give us terrible beatings. We knew that we were doing
something sinful, which we deserved to be punished for,
but the urges were too strong for either of us to resist.
Eventually I had to muster my courage to give him back to
his rightful owner, his wife, knowing without a shadow of
doubt that he was and always would be the true love of my
life.

All this time Mum and Dad and my brothers were not
giving up their plan to get Ahmed to England and told me
that I needed to appeal against the embassy's decision.
Ahmed used to phone the house from Pakistan, talking to
Dad and Ali first before they handed the phone on to me. I
would exchange a few words with Ahmed and then pretend
that I couldn't hear him because the line was breaking up.
He would still be shouting down the line, trying to be
heard, as I hung up. There was nothing I wanted to say to
him. I just wanted him out of my life for good. The months
kept on passing and it must have been driving poor Ahmed
crazy as he waited, having no idea what was happening on
the other side of the world while his own life in Lahore
went on exactly as it always had. The more time elapsed the
more I realised how terrible those few months with him

had been, and how impossible I would find it to go back there.

The machinery of the law grinds so slowly people's entire lives can ebb away as they wait for other people to make decisions that are going to affect everything but eventually the day of the appeal came round and Dad and I found ourselves sitting in front of a very nice judge. He listened to our solicitor putting the case for Ahmed to be granted a visa and I don't think he would have guessed from the way I talked that I was actually hoping he would say no.

'All your paperwork is in good order,' he said to me, 'you have done all the right things. Sadly, it is all to no avail because you are unable to do anything to rectify the damage your husband has done with his statements at the embassy in Pakistan. Not only did he give the answers that he did, he even repeated them and assured his questioner that he fully understood the questions he was being asked. It seems to me that your good nature has been taken advantage of here and I'm sorry to have to say that it is my opinion that this gentleman has married you solely in order to get into this country.'

I tried to look suitably sad at this revelation and not to smile, but actually I wanted to shout and cheer as he told me that there was no way he was going to overturn the previous decision. Ahmed was never going to be coming to

England for anything other than a visit, and the chances were he would have trouble even getting into the country at all. I thought that this must be the end of the whole, horrible story, but as soon as we got home the family were all talking about taking the appeal case to a lawyer in London who specialised in such things and trying again.

'But that will cost a fortune,' I protested. 'And he might not be able to make any difference in the end either.'

'We have to try, Saira,' Dad said. 'And we will find the money somehow.'

Not only was I horrified to think that I was still not safe, the idea that they would be pouring so much money away on such a lost cause was heartbreaking, especially when I was working so hard to try to improve the family's financial situation.

'But what happens if we pay this lawyer all this money,' I said, 'and he still doesn't manage to get the ruling overturned?'

'Then you will have to go and live in Pakistan,' Mum said and I felt all my hopes draining away, leaving a coldness and emptiness behind. I looked across at Dad and he simply nodded his solemn agreement.

Two days later the worst thing possible happened and news arrived that Ahmed's mother had died. He phoned to summon me back to the marital home. It was as if nothing had changed, as if I was still just his dutiful little wife who had been to Britain for a holiday and must now come back to fulfil her wifely duties as the grieving daughter-in-law. It seemed that it was only in my head that the marriage was over.

'You must go to them,' Dad told me. 'It is your duty.'

'What is the point of me going there?' I asked.

'He is your husband.' Dad spread his hands as if nothing more needed to be said. 'You can't just leave him there.'

'But he has clearly said he only married me to get into Britain,' I protested.

'No,' Mum interrupted. 'It was just because he isn't an educated person. He didn't understand the question properly, even if he thought he did.'

I couldn't disagree that Ahmed had shown how unintelligent he was by answering the question that way, but that didn't mean he hadn't meant what he said. Desperate to persuade them to change their minds I threw up all the arguments I had been storing in my head, but it didn't matter what I said to them, they believed they knew what the right thing was for me to do, and that was to return to my husband in his hour of need. I told myself that maybe it wasn't such a bad idea, that it would give me a chance to close this terrible chapter of my life once and for all, but that didn't do anything to quell the nerves that I felt as I pictured myself going back into my husband's home and into his bedroom.

10

The Escape

I returned to Pakistan with a heavy heart. My uncle met me at the airport and took charge of my passport as the men in families like mine always do, as if we women are like children who can't be trusted to keep anything safe. It was nice to see him but however friendly he was being I knew his job was to deliver me safely to my husband.

When we reached the house Ahmed was very welcoming and for a moment I wondered if perhaps he had realised that he would have to treat me better if he wanted to tempt me to stay. The moment we were alone, however, the affection immediately turned into a demand for sex and I realised that nothing had changed in the months we had been apart, except that his frustrations had increased and his needs had become even more urgent than before. I had been free of him for nearly a year and yet it seemed like no time had elapsed at all since the last time he had forced himself on me. In the darkness of the bedroom, as he snored contentedly next to me having had his brutal way, I knew I could not bear to live the rest of my life like this. In those few snatched hours with Aman I had seen what a relationship with a man could be like if it was the right man, and I knew there was nothing I could do to make Ahmed and me compatible. It wouldn't matter how hard I worked at the marriage, I would never be anything but miserable and I would be spending a large part of my life in physical pain, as well, always fearful of what was to come whenever my husband returned home from work, his hands stained with the blood of butchery.

Everyone in the family was talking as if it had been decided that I would stay in Pakistan now until Ahmed had succeeded in getting his visa for Britain. None of them seemed to think for a moment that he wouldn't be granted one eventually. I guess he never owned up to them about how badly he had messed up the interview, or perhaps he still didn't fully realise it himself. I protested half-heartedly from time to time, suggesting that I should go back to Britain ahead of him to earn some money, and then maybe the next appeal over Ahmed's visa application would work and he would be able to join me. I pointed out that I could send money back to him, which would help him with his visa application.

I didn't want to make him or his relatives angry with me unnecessarily, so I didn't push it too hard. I didn't want them to feel I was insulting them and their country by not wanting to be there. My mind was spinning all the time. I had now been married for nearly two years and I felt even more weighed down by it than I had at the beginning. I was constantly afraid of falling pregnant again, which made me even less keen to have sex with him every time he demanded it. Even though we had spent most of that time apart, the thought of living the rest of my life feeling like this was unbearable.

Desperately needing some space to think after a couple of weeks, I contacted my uncle and asked if I could go and stay with him and the family for a few days and he agreed without asking any more questions. Even though I didn't tell him every detail about what was going on in my life he knew that I was deeply unhappy, and he genuinely seemed to want to help. He behaved more like a father and brother to me than my real family did. Grandma had died a few months before so my uncles and aunts had now become the older generation. My aunt who was married to Ahmed's brother had always seemed much older than me, but she still seemed quite pleased to have another woman around the house for company, especially when she ventured out on her frequent shopping trips. I was never quite sure why she bothered to take me along as she nearly always left me trailing in her wake and hardly ever turned round to talk to me as she progressed from one shop to the next, fingering everything that the shopkeepers held out to her before rejecting it. Most of the time she didn't really want to buy anything, I think she just wanted an excuse to get out of the house. I could understand that feeling very well and was happy to go with her whenever she suggested an outing.

I had realised, as I walked around the streets behind her, both of us covered from head to toe, that this was how my life was going to be from now on if I didn't do something quickly. I might get respites when I was able to go back to visit my family in Britain or was allowed to stay with my uncles and aunts, but basically I was married now and nothing was going to change that fact unless I took my destiny into my own hands. Sooner or later I was bound to get pregnant again and once I had children I would be even less able to travel back and forth to Britain when I wanted; I would be as trapped as every woman in my family had been for hundreds of years. If I was going to escape I had to do it quickly and I had to do it alone because no one else, not even my uncle, would be willing to help me.

It was a big decision to make because to run away from a marriage that had been arranged as mine had by family members would be to dishonour everyone involved. No one else would want to be tainted with my disgrace, so I wouldn't be able to involve anyone else or ask anyone else for help. I didn't want to bring shame to my family, but I didn't intend to live the rest of my life enslaved to Ahmed either. I began to plot and plan how I might run away, constantly watching what went on around the house and waiting for opportunities.

I knew that the first thing I needed to do was get back to Britain because no woman stood a chance of escaping from their family in Pakistan. Once there I knew I would still have to disappear from sight, telling no one where I was. I was under no illusion how seriously the men in the family would take this and my life would be in danger from the moment I took any step towards freedom, but at least in Britain I stood a chance of getting help from the authorities, which I would never be able to hope for in Pakistan.

The first problem was that I didn't have my passport, which I would need to travel, or my return ticket, both of which were in the care of my uncle. I had no idea how I was going to find an excuse to ask for them until one of my half sisters announced she was planning to travel to England and needed to book her flight.

'Would you like me to book it for you when I am next shopping with Auntie?' I asked innocently.

She accepted the offer gratefully, her hands being full with her children. My uncle gave me permission to fetch her passport from his room and while I was in there I quickly slipped my own passport and return ticket down into the front of my dress and wrapped my shawl around me. My heart was crashing in my ears as I returned to the family. If I was caught doing this my uncle would see it as a betrayal of his trust in me on top of everything else and everyone would be suspicious of me from that moment on, never letting me out of their sight. I knew that if I didn't get away with this escape first time it would be a thousand times harder to do it again once they were all watching me.

Knowing that Auntie didn't speak English, I could be sure that she wouldn't understand what was happening if I booked my own return flight as well as my half sister's while we were in the travel agents. In the end she didn't even bother to come into the agency with me, preferring to go into the fabric shop next door and wait for me there. I booked my sister on to a flight a week later and I chose a flight for myself that was at a reasonable time in the evening in a couple of days' time. The booking-in time for the flight was at an hour when it would be possible for me to be out in the market with Auntie again, which I thought would give me a better chance of getting away than if I was at home.

My second problem was that I would need money for things like taxis or for extra charges once I got to the airport. I was not allowed to have any cash of my own, but I did have some gold jewellery which I had been given at my wedding. I told Auntie that I wanted to sell my jewellery to help Ahmed's family with some of his mother's funeral expenses. She seemed to think that was a perfectly reasonable thing for me to do and even took me to a shop that she thought would give me a fair price.

'Please don't tell Ahmed that you know I have sold the gold,' I said as we left the shop with the cash. 'He would be so embarrassed to think that you knew he had asked me to do that.'

'Of course,' she said. 'I understand.'

That evening my uncle remembered the passport and ticket that I had been given charge of.

'Do you have your sister's passport?' he asked and my heart missed a beat. I didn't want him to take it because he might notice that my papers were missing when he went back to his room with it.

'Yeah,' I said, trying to sound casual. 'I'll go and put it back in your room.'

He stared at me hard for a moment and I thought I must have given something away. 'Thank you for your help, Saira,' he said.

'You're welcome.'

I was able to breathe again as he returned to whatever he was doing and I took my sister's passport back to his room. For the next two days I was terrified every time my uncle came near me that he was going to tell me he had been looking through the family papers and noticed my passport and ticket were missing, but he gave no indication of suspecting anything. I kept my arms covered all the time so that Ahmed wouldn't notice my missing bracelets. During the day of the flight, when no one was watching me, I packed a small suitcase and hid it under the bed in case Ahmed came home unexpectedly and asked what I was doing. At lunchtime I casually suggested to Auntie that we should go out to the market that afternoon. The timing had to be right because I didn't want to be sitting around at the airport too long waiting for my plane in case the family came after me, but I also had to build in some time in case anything went wrong and I was delayed.

'OK,' she said. 'There are a few things I would like to look at.'

Just as we were about to leave I went to our room and pulled the suitcase out from under the bed. I had to carry it as if it was empty, even though it was heavy with my things.

'Why are you taking a suitcase?' she asked as we left the house.

'It's not a suitcase,' I said, as casually as I could manage. 'It's just a bag because there are quite a few things I want to get and I need to be able to carry them. Those plastic bags they give you in shops are no good for anything.'

To my relief she accepted my explanation without another thought and sailed off ahead of me down the street as usual. I trailed along behind like always, allowing her to get further and further into the market, struggling to make the suitcase look light in case anyone was watching. There was one store she particularly liked, which was stacked so high with produce it was easy to lose sight of someone as they browsed around. I waited till she got there, and the moment she started talking to the shopkeeper I turned and walked back out into the street. If I could find a way to get straight to the airport now I should be just about on time, as long as the plane hadn't been delayed or cancelled. I felt so frightened of being caught there was part of me that wished I had never started on the plan, but another part of me was excited at the thought of taking my fate into my own hands at last.

The street was crowded and it was hard to get through the people without banging into others with my case, but I didn't care as I pushed my way onwards, trying to move faster as I got further from the shop. The more people there were the more quickly I would be invisible to my aunt or anyone else she might send to find me. The case had become heavy as it banged into people's legs, making them shout at me angrily. I broke into a sweat inside my robes as I headed for a street corner where I knew taxi drivers waited for fares. I had heard terrible stories about women who had travelled alone in taxis and had ended up being driven out into the countryside where they were raped and killed. The police never seemed that bothered about investigating such crimes, probably thinking that any woman who travelled alone among strange men was asking for trouble anyway. All my experiences of men so far made me very able to believe such stories were true, but I had to risk it. I had no choice. I had to get to the airport fast and a taxi was my only option.

There were several cars waiting, the drivers standing around talking, some of them calling out to passers-by, trying to drum up business. As I approached I chose an older man who I guessed would be the safest bet, since he looked too fat to be able to chase me should I need to make a run for it.

'Take me to the airport,' I said in as commanding a voice as possible, pulling my scarf across my face so that he wouldn't see how young I was. His expression showed no emotion as he lumbered round to the driver's door and the other men watched me struggling into the backseat with my case without saying anything. As we set off the driver's eyes were on me in the rear-view mirror as often as they were on the road outside. It felt as if he was trying to stare through my scarf, but I pretended not to notice and only replied with grunts to his questions.

The airport came in sight but I still kept the scarf over my face, my eyes darting around, half expecting to see Ahmed or my uncle or even a policeman coming towards the taxi as it drew up. I got out, paid the driver and hurried into the terminal, anxious to get through security, where no one would be able to follow unless they had a ticket. There were a couple of hours to wait before boarding and I jumped every time an announcement came crackling over the tannoy system, expecting to hear my own name called out at any moment. If I was caught now the repercussions would be terrible and I wouldn't be able to expect any support from anyone in the family, men or women. There seemed to be policemen and soldiers everywhere I looked and I became convinced they were all searching for me as they wandered around in pairs, their eyes scanning the crowds. I kept my head down and my scarf up, grateful for all the other women doing the same, helping me to become invisible.

Finally my flight was called and as I walked through with my boarding pass it felt as if every eye in the place was staring at me, as if they all knew everything about me and were just teasing me, waiting till the last moment before telling me that I couldn't board, before asking me to step through some door into a side room where my uncle would be waiting to take me home.

Even once I was in my seat on the plane it seemed to take an age before the engines roared into life and we taxied towards the runway. When the stewardess leaned over me to check my belt was done up I averted my eyes and stared hard out of the window. She moved away to the next set of seats and the plane gathered speed.

At last we were in the air. I was safely off the ground of

Lahore, but now I had hours of worry ahead of me as I imagined the phone calls going through to the UK from Pakistan. They were bound to have realised I had gone by now. Even if they initially thought I had been abducted they would soon check if my passport and ticket were still in my uncle's room and when they found them gone they would remember I had left the house carrying a suitcase and would put all the pieces together. My aunt would then remember the cash that I had received for my jewellery. My own family would be furious and embarrassed to have lost face in front of Ahmed's family and the rest of the community. In their eyes they had already saved me from one disgrace by succeeding in marrying me off, now I had gone further than they would ever be able to tolerate. If my father and brothers got hold of me now, now that I had dishonoured them in front of my in-laws, they would certainly want to kill me.

The first leg of the flight only took me as far as Karachi, where there was a stopover of around five hours. Other passengers were going out into the city to meet friends and relatives while they waited, but there was no way I was going to risk that in case someone had guessed which plane I was on and was waiting for me on the other side of the barriers. They might even have informed the authorities and the passport control officers would be looking out for me.

'Is there somewhere I can sit and wait for my connection?' I asked a passing stewardess.

'You could sit there, if you want,' she said, pointing doubtfully to some uncomfortable-looking chairs. 'But it will be a long wait.'

She was right, but I didn't think I had any choice. As long as I stayed close to the planes I felt I was safe, guarded from my family by the many security channels of the airport. I sat and sweated away the hours until eventually my onward flight was called and I made my way back through to the plane. Finally I was leaving Pakistan.

Even though I was exhausted by the stress of the previous few days, I still only slept fitfully on the flight, my nerves strung so tight by the time we landed at Heathrow that I could hardly breathe. I was completely certain that my father or brothers would be at the airport by then, meeting every flight that came in from Pakistan in case I was on it. As I stepped off the plane I half expected them to be waiting at the door with the airline officials, ready to whisk me away. I knew they would want to kill me for what I had done, especially Ali with all his mad ideas about honour and pride. I knew that he had used violence against people who had crossed him because there had been trouble with the police, and I had seen what happened to Aman in front of my own eyes. The fact that I was his sister wouldn't stop Ali; in fact it might fuel his anger even further. I would never forget the cruel games both my brothers used to play with me when Mum and Dad left us alone as children.

Despite having been awake most of the night, thinking, I still had no real plan as to what to do next. I was walking like a zombie towards passport control. There was a long queue of tired people, lined up, waiting their turn to go through, and I joined the end of it, my mind whirring and my eyes darting around, alert for danger, expecting to find someone staring at me, or to see one of my brothers pointing me out to officials.

I shuffled to the front of the queue and the customs official stared at me threateningly as he leafed through the pages of my passport, asked a couple of questions, which I answered with my eyes to the floor, and then nodded for me to go through. I walked on to the luggage hall in a daze. This was my last chance. Once I was through the next set of doors I would emerge into the landside areas of the airport, unprotected from whoever might be waiting for me. I had taken my little suitcase on board as hand luggage, but I still hung around in the baggage reclaim area for half an hour as I tried to work out what to do. I was aware that the longer I left it, the more time my brothers would have to get to the airport and organise other people to watch the various exits. I needed to do something decisive.

There was a young Asian security woman not much

older than me hovering around the luggage carousels. She had a clipboard and seemed to be a manager of some sort. Everyone else working in the room was male and white and looked bad-tempered, apart from a couple of women with mops methodically polishing the floors, showing no interest in anything that was going on around them. Taking a deep breath, I stepped over to the young Asian woman.

'Excuse me,' I said, annoyed to hear my voice trembling when I was trying so hard to be cool. 'Can I speak to you?'

She looked suspicious for a moment and slightly annoyed to be interrupted from whatever it was she was supposed to be doing, but then seemed to decide that I was genuinely in need of help and lowered her clipboard to listen.

'I have run away from an arranged marriage in Lahore,' I gabbled my story out as quickly as possible for fear of losing her attention. 'My husband was cruel to me, but my family will be waiting for me on the other side of the barriers if I go through with everyone else. If they get hold of me, they will kill me.'

To my relief I saw her expression soften. She obviously understood exactly what I was talking about. Maybe she came from a family like mine too or had friends who had been forced into arranged marriages.

'Is there any other way I can get out of the airport?' I pleaded.

'Is that all your luggage?' she asked.

I nodded.

'OK, come with me.'

She led me through a small door, punching in a personal security code and bringing me out into an empty corridor on the other side. I had no idea if she was helping me or arresting me, but I had no one else to trust so I followed obediently.

'Where do you want to get to?' she asked.

I told her where I came from. Part of me was terrified of returning to the place where my family lived, but the thought of going to a completely strange city was even more frightening.

'I'll take you through to the coach station,' she said.

I knew there was a possibility that my brothers would have someone watching the coaches back to our city, but I couldn't think of another way of getting out of the area. I was just going to have to hope that they weren't that organised. They had only had one night to get to Heathrow and the chances that they would have thought of finding the coach station were reasonably slight, but my heart was still thumping so hard I thought I might faint as my saviour took me through the ticket office and loaded me on to a coach. The seats around me were crowded with other people returning home, all loaded down with bags and cases and the occasional household item that they must have been given or had bought cheap wherever they had been travelling.

'How much money do you have?' the girl asked.

'About forty pounds.'

'That won't be enough.'

She pulled out her purse and thrust all the notes from it into my hand. I tried to protest at such generosity from a stranger but she insisted I took it.

'Take my telephone number,' she said, writing it down for me. 'You can pay me back when you're able to. Let me know how you get on.'

She waited until the coach drew out to wave me goodbye and I felt overwhelmed that someone who knew nothing about me at all should have shown me so much kindness and understanding at my moment of need. But my troubles were nowhere near being over. I might be safely out of Pakistan and out of Heathrow, but where was I going to go next? And who was I going to ask to help hide me?

I knew that I couldn't risk asking anyone in my family to help, even the ones whom I believed would be sympathetic, like my sister-in-law. I knew that the men would be interrogating everyone, determined to hunt me down. I wanted to contact Aman, but what could he possibly have done? And if they ever found out he had assisted me in any way they would definitely have killed him. The only person

I could think of who I believed I could trust and who would have nothing to do with the community my family lived in was my old form teacher, Mrs Thomson. I hadn't seen her since I left school, but I still remembered how kind and understanding she had been to me. She was the only person at the school that I used to show my private sketchbook to and she used to tell me that I should go to art school and that maybe I could make a career out of designing fabrics.

As soon as I got off the bus I hurried to the taxi rank, my scarf pulled tightly over my face, not looking to left or right, and asked the driver at the front of the queue to take me to a hotel in an area on the other side of the city where I was sure none of my family would ever go. With the money that the young woman at Heathrow had given me, I had just enough for one night's lodgings. I decided I would try to make contact with Mrs Thomson in the morning, once the school switchboard was open.

11
Into Hiding

The hotel that the taxi driver took me to was one of those anonymous chains where there is just one person on reception and fast food is available in the restaurant next door. The room was small but clean. It had exactly the sort of anonymity I needed, and it felt good to be able to close and lock the door behind me and feel safe for a few hours, even though my brain was whirling around so fast I could hardly sleep that night. I had already been awake several hours, listening to other guests getting up for breakfast or setting off to work, by the time the school switchboard opened at eight o'clock and I made my call.

'Can I speak to Mrs Thomson?' I asked, recognising the headmistress's voice on the other end, even after all those years.

'She's not here at the moment,' she replied, suggesting I ring again between lessons in an hour or two. Having been waiting so long to make the call I felt deflated at being put off, but there was no alternative since I still hadn't been able to think of a single other person I would trust to go to for help.

Each minute dragged by as I waited and I knew I was going to have to be out of the hotel room by twelve. I tried putting the television on to pass the time but I found the noise too distracting. I wanted to concentrate every brain cell I had on solving my problems. I preferred the quiet so I could listen for any voices outside the room. I knew the chances of anyone finding me there were almost non-existent, but I still couldn't shake off the fear. I phoned the school again at the exact moment the headmistress had told me and Mrs Thomson came on the line. I told her my name and she remembered me immediately, even though it was more than three years since I had seen her. She had always seemed very fond of our class and had actually cried when we all left. I told her very briefly what the problem was and that I needed help.

'I've just got to go into another lesson in a minute,' she said. 'Let me make a couple of phone calls and then I'll ring you back.'

When she rang she told me to meet her after school at three-thirty so that she could take me somewhere safe. That left me with three hours to fill after checking-out time at the hotel. Wrapping my scarf round my face, still clutching my little suitcase, I paid my bill and left. I didn't know where else to go, so I walked round and round the nearby park for an hour or two before plucking up the courage to ring my sister-in-law. I felt so alone I craved to talk to someone friendly and familiar, to remind myself that I wasn't completely alone in the world.

'Where are you?' she asked in a whisper.

'I'm in the park,' I said, feeling the tears rising up at the sound of her voice. 'Can you get away for a few minutes to meet me?'

'I'll try. Where are you exactly?'

I told her, even though I was frightened of leading my brothers to me. I trusted her not to deliberately give me away, but they might well be watching her. I found some trees I could stand behind and watch for anyone suspicious. She must have made some excuse to get out of the house because I spotted her on the other side of the park half an hour later, her rounded stomach told me she was expecting again. I waited until I was sure she hadn't been followed before emerging from my hiding place and going over to her.

'How's Sulaiman?' I asked almost immediately.

'He's fine.' She brushed aside my query about her son, obviously more interested in finding out about my adventures. 'He misses you. What happened in Lahore?'

'I ran away,' I said, not really wanting to go into too much detail, my eyes constantly moving around the park in case anyone was watching us. 'What's happening at home?'

'When the call came through to say that you'd disappeared, your dad went mad. He thought your mum's family had done something to you. He thought maybe your uncle had killed you.'

'Why?'

'I don't know exactly. Something to do with revenge for the way his family treated your mum in the past? Or because you kept leaving Ahmed on his own and obviously wanted to divorce him. Everyone was shouting and arguing and accusing everyone else.'

The fact that Dad even considered that such a thing might be a reasonable assumption said a lot about the way families like ours behave. It also suggested that he had an uneasy conscience himself about the way he had allowed Mum to be used like a slave when she came to Britain. I knew it would not be out of the question for a young girl like me, who was causing embarrassment for her family, to simply disappear and for the family never to give away what had happened to her, and I could also understand how he could think that I might have been murdered in revenge for the way he had treated Mum in the past.

'Ali guessed you had probably run away almost immediately,' she went on. 'He went straight down to Heathrow. He was meeting every flight. When you hadn't arrived after twenty-four hours or so he decided you must still be out there. He got a flight out to Lahore to try to track you down himself. He's so angry he swears he's going to kill you when he finds you. I hoped the fact I was pregnant again would please him and calm him down, but it hasn't made any difference at all.'

Months later I was shown pictures of my brother out in Lahore on that mission, armed with what looks to me like a machine gun. There is no question that he was prepared to kill me at that stage if he could have got me on my own.

My sister-in-law could only stay talking for a few minutes, fearful that she would be missed at home and they might guess that she was meeting me, which would certainly have earned her a severe beating. I felt so alone as I watched her hurry away, my only contact with my previous life disappearing over the horizon. I went back to walking around the park until it was time to go to the school.

Mrs Thomson was waiting for me at the gates and took charge of the situation in her usual no-nonsense manner. It was such a relief to feel that someone knew what to do. She put me in her car and drove me to the office of a refuge for women that she had phoned earlier. Even though the refuge was located in quite a rough area, the workers who met me were very sympathetic and nice, and Mrs Thomson left once she was satisfied that they were taking care of me, promising to come back and see me in a few days. I was so grateful to her. Like the woman at Heathrow, she had put herself out to help me when I was no longer her responsibility, and such acts restored my faith in my fellow humans a little.

Once I had told them my whole story the refuge workers agreed to find me a room in their centre, which was a great big house a few streets from their office. The matron of the house took me round and showed me to a bed-sitting room upstairs before leading me down for a guided tour of the ground floor.

'That's the main lounge for everyone to share,' she said, gesturing towards a door, 'and this is the kitchen.'

The kitchen was a nice clean room with lots of cupboards for everyone to share. The matron then had to go, and after unpacking my little case I ventured nervously back down to the lounge to see what the other residents were like. As I came through the door the first person I saw was one of our white neighbours, who often talked to my mother at the local shop where she worked behind the counter. She was sitting on the other side of the room with her children. Our eyes met and I could see she was as shocked as I was. I tried to compose myself and went over to say hello.

'What are you doing here?' she asked.

'I've run away,' I said. 'Why are you here?'

'My husband beat me up, so they are letting me stay here until I can get somewhere to live on my own with the children.'

As soon as it was polite to end the conversation I hurried back to the matron's office.

'I can't stay here,' I said, struggling not to let the feeling of panic overwhelm me.

'Why not?' she asked, obviously surprised that I had changed so completely from seeming so relieved and grateful a few minutes earlier to be somewhere safe.

'One of our neighbours is in that room. She and my family are really close friends and I can guarantee she will ring Mum and tell her where I am.'

'OK,' she said, able to see how scared I was. 'It's too late to do anything tonight but we'll move you somewhere else in the morning.'

'You don't understand,' I said, shaking uncontrollably. 'I can't stay here tonight. She's probably calling Mum already. That's how close they are.'

'All right,' she said, picking up the phone. 'Let's see if we can find somewhere else for you to go.'

She rang round a number of people while I waited in her office, terrified that any moment there would be a knock on the door and Dad or Ali would be on the doorstep, shouting and throwing punches at anyone who tried to stop them taking me away. About an hour later she had managed to find a place for me in a refuge about an hour's train ride away. Thanking her profusely, I hurried upstairs to repack my battered little case. She told me someone would meet me when I got to the station at the other end but I felt very lost and alone as the almost empty train rattled me off to an unknown destination. Yet again I was putting my fate in the hands of more strangers.

The Sikh girl who was waiting for me as I emerged from the station must have been able to see how scared I was from the look on my face and tried to calm me down, assuring me that no one back home would be able to find out where I was now. She drove me to a refuge that was similar to the one I had just left, although a little more homely. The other girls in there were very friendly and welcoming, all of them in similar situations to me, trying to find ways to escape from families who were forcing them to do things they didn't want to, or in hiding from abusive partners. There was one beautiful little Indian girl who had been brought over to England by her husband, who then decided he didn't like her after all and kicked her out on to the streets with nothing but the clothes she was wearing. She looked so frail, always sitting in her room, reading books. It was hard to understand how anybody could find a fault with her. There was another lovely, bubbly girl from Bangladesh whose husband had brought her over and treated her as a slave for his family. He would then openly date other women and tell her about them. In the end he poured petrol over her and tried to set light to her. Listening to all their stories it was comforting to know that I was not alone, that I shared common experiences with the others living around me, but frightening to think how widespread the abuse of Asian women was.

It was a relief to be able to talk openly and honestly about things that were usually unspeakable within traditional Asian families, and to be living among nice people who didn't expect anything of me. Over the following days I found myself relaxing and fitting in without any trouble. I wasn't making any plans and had no idea what I was going to do next with my life. I went from day to day, simply existing. Some days the time hung very heavy as I sat around with the other girls and I did find myself getting bored, but that was infinitely preferable to feeling frightened all the time. Some of the others would go out into the city and meet boys and lead quite normal social lives, but I didn't know how to go about doing that. Every time I had tried to lead a normal Western life in the past it had gone horribly wrong, so it seemed easier to stay within the safe surroundings of the refuge. The only rule was that we had to be in by ten at night, but I never wanted to go out anyway. The refuge was homely enough, with sofas and a television in the lounge, so I stayed there most evenings. I finally had the freedom that I had craved all through those years when my family wouldn't allow me to go out or meet whoever I wanted or wear what everyone else was wearing, but I didn't take advantage of it. I didn't know how to, and I no longer wanted to anyway.

They gave me enough money to buy some essentials like clothes. I went shopping with my key worker, and I was allowed to buy whatever I wanted, but I still chose baggy tops that covered my bum and long skirts that hid my legs so I didn't attract attention to myself. I did, however, finally get taken to a proper underwear shop and was measured for a bra that fitted for the first time ever. It felt so good after so many years of discomfort.

After a few weeks, however, I realised I would have to find something to fill the long hours if I wasn't going to end up a total recluse for the rest of my days, allowing myself to be defeated by life and by the men in my family in the same way as so many other Asian women did. I also wanted some spending money to buy a few extras, so I mustered all my courage and applied for a job in a local family factory, working on a sewing machine just like I had watched Mum doing all my life. I got the job easily and each day I would go to work first thing in the morning and return to the refuge at night, still not wanting to go anywhere else. It was a nice, friendly environment in the factory, the monotony of the work and the conversation-killing buzz of the machines giving me time to be alone with my thoughts while at the same time providing me with a bit of distraction and variety, and some money at the end of the week.

After a couple of months I realised that some of the sadness I felt every day was because I was missing being part of a real family. I might have hated what my family had done to me, but I still loved them all as individuals, and it was hard to think of them all going on with their lives at home without me, as if I was already dead to them. The person I missed the most was my nephew. I kept thinking about how he was growing up and how I was missing all the changes he would be going through. I longed to be able to hold him in my arms and feel him clinging to my neck, covering my face with kisses and making me laugh. I didn't want to go back to my life in Pakistan, and I didn't want to be living as Ahmed's wife in Britain either, but I did want to be part of the family again.

I knew that my parents and brothers would still be angry with me and might stay that way for the rest of their lives, and it was a terrible thought that I might never again be reconciled with them all. My key worker had heard from the people at the first refuge I went to that, just as I had predicted, Mum had received a call from our neighbour, telling her the address. My brother Ali had turned up the same night, banging on the door and demanding that they turn me over to him. I'm convinced that if he had managed to get to me that night he would have killed me. In the end the matron had to call the police to have him removed. If he felt that strongly then, I couldn't imagine that he would have changed his opinion of me in just a few months.

The refuge was willing to keep me there for six months without asking any questions, allowing things to settle down before reviewing the situation and trying to work out if there was a way of reconciling me either with my family or with another community. Ideally, they always wanted to reunite the women in their care with their immediate families and resolve the problems that had led to them having to escape in the first place. If that wasn't possible they would start to look for ways to make the women more independent by moving them into outside accommodation so they could restart their lives on their own.

After four months they asked me if I thought it would be a good idea for them to phone Dad up and find out what his views on my behaviour were now, and maybe to try to explain the situation from my point of view now that some time had elapsed and he'd had time to think things through. I couldn't see any harm in it, as long as he wasn't allowed to find out where I was living, although I can't say I was optimistic about their chances of winning him over.

'We've spoken to him,' the social worker told me the next day, 'and he says he wants to talk to you. He seemed quite reasonable and keen to make peace.'

Just hearing those words stirred emotions inside me that I had been repressing for months. I had quite expected that he would shout at them, saying he wanted nothing more to do with me, that as far as he was concerned I was dead to him. I was shocked to find I had misjudged him so. I realised there was still a danger that it might be a trick, that he would try to lure me back home and would then punish me the moment no one was watching, but at least he had opened up the possibility that perhaps one day I could go back.

'Would you be willing to talk to him on the phone?' she asked.

'OK,' I said, feeling as nervous as if I had just been asked to get up on a stage and make a speech.

I had no idea what sort of reaction I would get when he heard my voice. Would he be unable to control his anger and shout abuse at me down the line? Would he tell me how bad I was and how much I had let the family down? Would he insist that I went back to my husband?

The social worker dialled the number for me and I avoided her eyes in case I started to cry. I could hear the phone ringing a few times before it was picked up and I could hear Dad's voice answering.

'I have Saira for you, Mr Ahmed,' she said. 'She would like to talk to you.'

'Hello,' I said, shyly, as the social worker handed me the phone. 'Dad?'

'Whatever you want, Saira,' he said without even saying hello, 'I'll do.'

He sounded tired, as if he had no more energy to fight

or to keep up appearances, as if he just wanted it all to be over. Hearing his familiar voice made the tears come to my eyes and I couldn't trust myself to speak. I kept my eyes down.

'If you want to wear a skirt,' he went on when I didn't answer, 'that is OK. If you want to meet boys, that is up to you. Wherever you want to go to work, it is up to you. You are a grown-up, you must make your own decisions. If you want to divorce Ahmed that is OK too. All I want is to have my daughter safely back home.'

I felt so much love for him at that moment, unlike anything I had felt before. I could tell that he meant it, that he really wanted me to come back. It seemed that the months of separation had made him realise he missed me as much as it had made me realise I missed them. I doubt if he had ever believed that I would have the nerve to run away from them in the way I had. He, like most men from his background, had believed he had absolute power over the women in his family. By defying him I had shown him how much he would risk losing if he didn't hold out an olive branch. A lot of men would have refused to climb down, and I loved him for being willing to admit that perhaps I had a point. What I had wanted to hear him say most of all, of course, was that if I wanted a divorce I could have one, and he had said it. If he meant what he said then I had won.

'I'm ready to go home now,' I said quietly to the social worker once I had hung up the phone.

'Are you sure?' she asked. 'Don't rush. Let's talk about it more. Take your time before you decide.'

Although I really wanted to run straight home I knew she was right. I still couldn't be sure what would happen once I was back in the house. I certainly didn't know if my brothers felt the same way as Dad. I was willing to be guided by the experts, people who had experience with girls in my situation. We had several meetings at the refuge, which were almost like counselling sessions.

'Is there anyone from the family that you would like to see first,' my social worker asked, 'before you commit to going back?'

'I would love to see my little nephew,' I said. 'I've missed him so much.'

'Well then,' she said, 'let me try and arrange that as a first step.'

12
Going Home

Over the previous few months, whenever I had some spare money from my work at the garment factory, I had bought little toys for Sulaiman, without even knowing if I would ever see him again. I had hardly been aware that I was doing it. It was as if I was subconsciously telling myself that I was still part of the family, keeping the hope alive that I would be seeing him again soon, before he was too old to appreciate the things I had bought him. I had ended up with a big black bag full of stuff.

The social worker contacted my sister-in-law who was heavily pregnant with her second child, and they agreed a time and place when she would be able to take Sulaiman out of the house without being detected. I was still nervous, worried that my brother might suspect something and follow her. I knew that one of my old schoolfriends had become a police officer and I wondered if she would be willing to help us out. Mrs Thomson had been staying in touch while I was in the refuge, checking every couple of weeks or so that I was doing all right, and she got the girl's number for me. I rang her and asked if she would be willing to meet me off the train in her uniform and just be around for me in case anything went wrong.

My other big fear was that Sulaiman would have forgotten me during the months that we were apart; after all they were a big percentage of his short life. I needn't have worried because he recognised me the moment he saw me approaching with my policewoman friend and came running over, arms outstretched, shouting my name. He had changed so much it made me realise how much time I had lost.

'Ali thinks I am out for a driving lesson,' my sister-in-law told me, 'so I can only stay for an hour.'

We went to a cafe at the station, huddling in a corner with the policewoman hovering in the background, while I caught up on all the news and gave Sulaiman some of the things I had bought for him. It felt so good to be with someone from the family again.

'Things are better at home now,' my sister-in-law told me. 'Everyone is missing you and wants you back.' Despite her reassuring words I noticed she was constantly glancing at her watch, obviously nervous that she would stay too long and get into trouble with Ali. I found her nervousness was rubbing off on me. The moment the hour was up she stood up to go. Sulaiman, however, was not keen to be parted from his gift-bearing aunt now that he had found her again.

'We have to go now, Sulaiman,' his mother insisted and I could tell she was getting worried.

Sulaiman immediately started to scream and shout, clinging on to me and refusing to let go. I had never seen a tantrum like it. Watching his mother prising his fingers off me and pulling him away, desperate not to be delayed and horrified by the attention that Sulaiman's screams were drawing to our presence there, I felt that I was being torn in half. I really wanted to go back to the family with them, to be part of something bigger than just myself again, but at the same time I didn't want to return to living in fear of the men in the family, having to rush around like my sister-in-law, terrified that they would find out what I was doing and be angry with me. I had tasted freedom and although it wasn't as wonderful as I had hoped, bringing with it a fair bit of loneliness, the thought of losing it again was a far worse option. Eventually Sulaiman had to be physically carried away, and I hurried off in the opposite direction to find a train back to the safety of the refuge while I tried to work out the best thing to do.

I couldn't stop thinking about Sulaiman as I stared out of the window at the passing scenery on the journey back, or when I was lying awake in my bed that night. All I had wanted to do when he had cried was hold him in my arms and comfort him and promise to be there for him every day, coming and going in his life like all his other relatives. It was beginning to seem inevitable that I would have to pluck up my courage sooner or later and go back to face whatever fate my brothers might have in store for me. I couldn't continue living in the wilderness forever, however safe it might be. A few days later, having spent hours bent silently over the sewing machine at work agonising about the right thing to do, I told the social workers at the refuge that I was ready to go home.

'Are you sure?' they asked.

'Yes. Please can you make the necessary arrangements?'

They agreed to do what I asked, and even offered to come with me on my return to make sure I was safe and to show my brothers that they were watching out for me, but I said I would be OK.

'We'll come round to the house tomorrow,' they promised, 'just in case. And we'll stay in touch for as long as you need us.'

Dad was waiting for me at the station when I arrived back with the few worldly goods I had acquired over the previous few months. He didn't seem to know what to say to me and I was surprised by how much he had aged since I last saw him. He had always been such a powerful figure in my life, but now I could see that he was turning into an old man, worn out by life and by his own children.

We took a bus home, and when we walked into the

house, with me still carrying the battered little suitcase I had escaped from Lahore with, family life seemed to be going on as normal and no one said a word to me about where I had been or what had happened to me since I last saw them all. It was as if I had just popped out to the shops and nothing had changed while I was away, meals still had to be made, clothes washed and money had to be earned. I was relieved in some ways that no one was making a big fuss, but I also felt this was more evidence that they all thought very little of me.

Despite them pretending that nothing was different, I could see it was. Mum had aged just as much as Dad, as if the strain of the previous few months had worn her down, coming on top of everything else in her life. I felt a spasm of guilt at the thought that I might have been the cause of more problems for them and vowed to myself that I would make it up to them as long as they allowed me to stay in Britain with them.

The atmosphere was so different to the sense of joy and optimism that had pervaded everything during the weeks of my brother's wedding, a time when everyone had been so lively and joyful. It felt now as if the cares of the world had descended on us all and my homecoming didn't seem to be doing anything to lighten the mood. There was no happiness left in the house, everything was dull and dreary apart from Sulaiman. He toddled about from room to room, constantly talking as the new baby, a little girl, slept peacefully in her pram. Mum seemed particularly glum, and I assumed it was because Ahmed had come from her side of the family, so she was feeling the disgrace of what I had done even more than Dad. I expect Dad had been giving her a hard time as well, blaming her family for what had happened as they were the ones who had arranged the marriage, especially in the early days when he believed my uncle had killed me.

As I sat down in the front room, with Mum at her sewing machine and Dad on the sofa beside me, I became aware of the bad smell coming from the trainers that I had been wearing virtually nonstop since leaving Lahore. It reminded me of all the years that I had been so self-conscious about my body odours, so certain that I would never be attractive to anyone.

'Do you want to go for a shower?' Dad asked, which made me think I wasn't the only one who had noticed. I didn't tell him that I had already had one before I left the refuge that morning. It was as if my feet were determined to show me up, however hard I might try to be a lovely fragrant young lady and a credit to my parents.

I did as he suggested and by the time I returned downstairs from the bathroom word must have gone round the neighbourhood that I was back because there was a steady stream of relatives coming round to take a look at the girl who had dared to run away and to bring disgrace to her family name.

'Where have you been?' one of the bolder cousins asked eventually. 'Where did you go?'

'Nowhere,' I shrugged, not wanting to be an object of interest for a moment longer than I had to. I now wanted to melt invisibly back into the family and get on with my life as if the whole thing had never happened, and I didn't want to give anyone any details about my private problems. Although I didn't regret what I had done because the thought of being in Pakistan with Ahmed was unbearable, I was still not proud to have failed at my marriage and to have caused my parents so much heartache and shame.

Asif was away in Pakistan at the time of my return and Ali was out of the house when I arrived. I assumed he must have been told that I was due back that day and was making a point by not being there, but when he came in and saw me he seemed shocked and made no attempt to hide his disgust, so perhaps Dad had not dared to tell him that I was being forgiven. The anger blazed from Ali's eyes as he looked at me, as if he wanted to kill me there and then with his bare hands. I shrank back, mesmerised by his eyes, too frightened even to make a run for the door.

'What's she doing here?' he demanded to know.

'I brought her home,' Dad replied quietly. 'You need to say nothing to her.'

Although Ali strutted around like he owned the world, he would still always be respectful of Dad's wishes whatever he might secretly think of him, but he didn't pretend to be pleased that I was there. As far as he was concerned I had dishonoured him and his family and he was never going to forgive me. Without another word he stamped upstairs to his bedroom. Dad must have sensed how frightened I was of what Ali might do because he stayed in all evening (which he would never normally have done) to make sure nothing happened to me.

Over the following days Ali couldn't even bring himself to sit in the same room as me. There was nothing I could do to change the situation apart from wait for his mood to improve. Eventually he seemed to grow used to the fact I was there and bored with the effort of avoiding me when we were all living in such close quarters. Although he still didn't speak to me or look at me, after a couple of weeks he did at least stay in the same room as me from time to time, but even then he still couldn't bear it when he saw Sulaiman coming near me, ordering him away angrily. Being such a small child he didn't pick up on the warning signs and kept answering back.

'I want to go to Auntie,' he protested, blissfully unafraid of his father.

'No,' he shouted, making him jump and burst into tears. 'Don't go to her.'

It was as if he feared I would infect his son with my wicked, disrespectful ways. I didn't want him to have to be shouted at and the first time it happened I ran out of the room and went upstairs, weeping miserably into my pillow. After that I was careful not to encourage him to come to me whenever Ali was around. It was impossible to relax whenever he was there and I continued to feel that if Ali could have had his own way he would have liked to see me dead.

When Mum eventually mellowed enough to speak to me properly rather than just talking at me all the time, I asked her what I could do to win Ali over and to persuade him to forget the past. Up till then she had seemed to be studiously avoiding mentioning anything remotely personal.

'You don't realise what a terrible thing you have done,' she said, allowing all her pent-up grievances at the way I had disgraced her family to pour out. 'I suggest you apologise to Ali and beg his forgiveness. Then perhaps he will begin to accept you as his sister again.'

Although her tone made me bristle with unspoken indignation, I knew she was right and that I would have to be the one to apologise, even though there was part of me that wanted to shout at the top of my voice that it hadn't been my fault that I had been married off to a man I didn't love, that if anyone should be apologising it should be the family members who had decided to consign me to such a grim fate. I knew that if I became confrontational it would only drive Ali to even greater anger and we would never find a solution, perhaps remaining enemies for the rest of our lives. Mustering all my courage I went to see him in his room the next day, tapping politely on the door and waiting to be allowed in. He said nothing, just stared at me and waited to find out why I had dared to interrupt his privacy. I told him that I was sorry and begged him to forgive and forget because there was nothing I could do to undo the harm I had caused. I almost choked on every word, but he wasn't going to allow me to get away with it even then, almost spitting at me as he repeated everything Mum had said about disgracing the family, cataloguing my sins and listing all the ways in which I had let them and their god down. At the end of what felt like an interview I left the room in tears, partly out of frustration over all the things I had wanted to say but had had to hold in. In the following weeks, however, Ali's attitude towards me seemed to soften. Perhaps he felt that he had defeated me and proved his point and could therefore relax a little.

The first thing I needed to do was get back to work and bring in enough money to pay for my keep. I didn't want to be a financial burden to my parents after everything else I had put them through. I was aware that Ali was not contributing any money towards the family, although everyone seemed to be avoiding talking about exactly why that might be. The man who owned the sandwich bar offered me back my job, which meant that I became the main breadwinner of the family again, although it didn't earn me any respect. Every Friday I would come home with my pay packet and Mum would insist that I gave it to her unopened. If I opened it on the way home and took out a fiver for something I needed she would be furious.

'Do you not trust me with your money?' she would demand to know.

I didn't mind doing that at first. I knew the family had to eat and pay their bills. I was so happy to be away from Ahmed and to be allowed to live even this much of an independent life while still being with my family that I didn't care what happened to my money. I was enjoying working in the sandwich bar and the owner was very nice to me. He owned several different outlets and so he was often somewhere else and started leaving me in charge whenever he was out. It was no big deal because there were only ever two or three of us there and the others were happy to just get on with their jobs making the sandwiches and serving the customers. Then one evening he asked me to stay behind after the shop closed.

'This isn't my only business, you know,' he said, sitting me down and giving me a free Cherry Coke.

'I know you have other sandwich bars,' I said, wondering what he was getting at.

'The sandwich bars are only part of it.' He seemed to be enjoying telling me of his empire and seeing the surprise on my face.

'Really?' I said, genuinely surprised. I was impressed but still not sure why he was telling me.

'I run a catering company that does events like weddings and corporate lunches. Sometimes I have two or three different events running at the same time so I need people I can rely on to manage each one. Would you be interested in a job like that?'

It sounded terrifying, but when he told me the hourly rate I realised that if I accepted I would be earning twice what I was earning in the sandwich bar, plus there would be lots of opportunities to earn overtime by working late, or at weekends, or starting early.

'OK,' I said, 'if you think I can do it.'

The next day he gave me a uniform to wear and I was thrown straight in at the deep end, organising a cocktail party for some business people in a company boardroom. I was so scared my hands were shaking most of the time, but once I got going I discovered that everything was pretty much down to common sense. It was just a question of making sure the people preparing the food and the waiters and waitresses all did their jobs properly. I had spent enough years on the receiving end of employers' instructions to know how to be bossy if I was given permission. To start with I found it hard telling other people what to do, especially as they all knew more about the business than I did, but I persevered and I quite surprised myself with how well it went. My boss told me he was pleased with me and wanted me to take on bigger jobs. Before long I was working virtually every day of the week and often not getting home till late at night, having left before it was light in order to be at some venue or other to oversee the preparation of food and to check on deliveries.

Even after my apology Ali never fully approved of me. My sister-in-law was a dutiful, old-fashioned wife who obeyed his every order without question and I think he was worried that I might infect her with my dangerous ideas about women being allowed to live independent lives. Men like Ali could see that things were changing and their power bases in their families were being eroded by women like me, but as the months passed he appeared to accept that there was nothing he could do about it. He seemed to become more tolerant of my (increasingly infrequent) presence in the house, although he never showed me any affection, never laughed or joked with me as he sometimes had when we were younger. Maybe he was also haunted by memories of all the times he had behaved inappropriately towards me when I was a child and decided to blame me for leading him astray in some way. Or maybe he already had bigger and more shameful things in his own life to worry about by then and I simply wasn't important enough to bother about.

Although none of us knew the full extent of it by then, Ali's life was changing for the bad. Because of my innocence of the ways of the world it was a while before I realised what was happening and just how dangerously far he was straying from the straight and narrow. The rest of us never knew what he or Asif were up to when they were out of the house and I assumed they were just working hard in order to try to support themselves and get into a position where they would have enough money to help Mum and Dad support our many relatives back in Lahore. Gradually I picked up little snippets of information from other people whom I met through work or who dropped by the house. Everyone seemed to be too embarrassed to come right out about what they knew, but a picture was building up almost without me realising it. I learned that Ali had grown impatient with his job at the takeaway shop and wanted to earn his money more quickly and easily. Different people told me he was spending a lot of his nights working in the local clubs, although no one ever seemed to want to say exactly what he did there. All we knew was that some days he did seem to have a lot of money, and usually in cash, but that he still seemed to be getting into debt. He would act strangely a lot of the time, but it was several years before any of us realised it was because he was taking drugs and that the money he was making was coming from dealing. There is no doubt I was very naive about it all, but then I had never had any experience of that world. Ali had always acted strangely around me anyway so I took little notice of the clues that were mounting up.

The strangest thing about it, now that I have the benefit of hindsight, was that the more Ali indulged in drink and drugs the more rigid he became about his religious beliefs, particularly when it came to anything to do with the women in the family. He talked all the time about 'the honour of the family' when all the time he was dealing and taking drugs, drinking alcohol and betraying his wife by going out with other women and prostitutes.

The use of drugs and the drink may have gone against all my brother's religious beliefs, but they dulled his conscience and allowed him to keep sinning, while at the same time making him more judgemental of the behaviour of others. The guiltier he felt at his fall from his position as an honourable man in the community, the more he needed the substances that were causing his fall. It was as if the dilemma was driving him mad, and as his debts mounted up he started to pull all of us down with him.

Mum didn't finally admit that her beloved eldest son was going to the bad until she started catching him stealing things from the house to sell, like all her gold jewellery or the hi-fi from his room. She then became angry with him as well as disappointed, which would start the accusations and recriminations flying back and forth between them.

'You never loved me,' my brother would yell as she nagged him about his bad ways. 'All you ever did was beat me when I was little. I am what you made me.'

I was shocked to hear such things because I had always believed he was her favoured child, being the first boy, but I understood exactly why he might feel that way because the beatings and punishments we received from both of our parents were the most vivid memories from my childhood as well. I don't think Mum was capable of showing her love for any of her children; all her affection seemed to be saved for her own brothers and sisters back in Lahore. I never remember her cuddling us when we cried or stroking our heads if we were sick or couldn't sleep, or providing any of those little maternal gestures which make a child feel safe and loved. Perhaps she was too tired all the time, and too taken up with the day-to-day struggle for survival to have any strength left for shows of affection. I'm sure there were a hundred reasons from her own past for the way she treated us, but that was still the way it was.

More and more often as time passed and Dad became less active, it seemed to fall to me to sort out the problems that other members of the family caused. As I became more confident and more willing to speak up both Mum and Dad seemed to look to me for answers to problems rather than the other way round, as if the fact that I had been born and brought up in Britain made me more capable of finding my way around the system. I also seemed to be the only one who ever had any money when some new debt needed paying urgently. When Ali took my father's car without permission, for instance, and smashed into another driver, it was me who had to pay for the repairs to the other car in order to stop the irate driver going to the police or making an insurance claim (which would have shown that Ali wasn't insured to drive that night). Every day seemed to bring a new crisis and new expense that would drive my mother mad with worry and force her to come to me to tell me that I had to do something. Sometimes it felt as if I was the parent rather than the youngest child.

When he came back from Pakistan Asif was just as useless to Mum and Dad as Ali. He too was married by then and had produced two children quite quickly, so he constantly needed money. He never bothered to work, just hanging around the same clubs that Ali was involved with, socialising with all the same useless people. Neither of them was able to earn enough to support their lifestyles, even when Ali was dealing quite large amounts of drugs he was still totally broke. And so Ali resorted to acts of petty crime like stealing cars or breaking into warehouses at night while Asif would live off benefits and scrounge from Mum and Dad. They were both endlessly borrowing money off the rest of us to repay whichever debtors were becoming the most impatient and, in Ali's case, threatening. Neither Mum or Dad could afford to spare any money but still they gave in, running up more debts of their own in the process. My father would sit with his head in his hands, despairing of both of them, but he still gave them whatever he could, and borrowed more when his own wages weren't enough. They were his sons and it seemed sons always had to be given what they asked for, however undeserving they might be.

More and more frequently the police came knocking on the door looking for Ali, and it wasn't long before he started getting caught for a variety of things and began serving prison sentences. Mum and Dad then had to find the money for us all to go and visit him at weekends, wherever he was taken to, and they would buy him whatever he asked for at the same time as indulging Asif. Ali's prisons could be as far away as the Isle of Wight, which meant the rail fares would sometimes use up all of my week's wages. At a time when most of their friends were finding that their sons were starting to support them, Mum and Dad were actually having to pay more to look after their sons' responsibilities and support their grandchildren. Neither of my parents was good with money and they kept getting into debt with the wrong people as well, making things worse because then they had to pay interest too.

My brothers' private lives became more and more complicated, both of them fathering children by other women, all of which then had to be funded by the family in order to keep the women quiet. Because they were boys Dad couldn't accept that any of this was my brothers' own fault. Most of the time he blamed Mum for not bringing them up properly, although all through their marriage she had only ever done what he told her.

'The kids from my first marriage haven't turned out like this,' he would say, completely ignoring the fact that he was the one who chose to betray his first wife by leaving her and marrying my mother.

If anything was to blame for the way we all turned out I think it was the harsh discipline that Dad handed out when we were young, but maybe we were just destined to follow the paths we chose. His first children were brought up mostly in Pakistan, exposed to only one culture, always knowing their place in the world. My brothers and I never really knew who we were. Were we British or were we Pakistani? Should we behave like our families in Lahore had behaved for hundreds of years, or like the British people we had lived among during our childhoods? Sometimes it seemed to me that Ali resorted to drugs to forget about the rest of his life, to forget that his personal life in particular, was in such a mess and to forget that he and Asif were still at the bottom of the economic pile, no matter how much they struggled to rise.

My boss continued to be pleased with me and promoted me several times. Since each promotion meant more money, I always accepted, although I was aware that some of the other people he now employed weren't so happy about taking orders from someone as young as me. It was no longer like working in the sandwich bar where no one was ambitious or worried about their own career. I now had a job that other people wanted.

'Don't worry about it,' my boss said when I mentioned the ill-feeling some of the others were showing towards me. 'They'll get used to you. People like to grumble about their bosses. You're doing a good job, they will realise that.'

I might have been successful at work, but at home Mum was still treating me as if I was a child, always criticising, always complaining about Dad, always blaming me for anything that was wrong in her life. I understood that she'd had a hard time, and I understood that I had added to her burdens by running away from my marriage, but there was nothing I could do about that now. I was working hard, supporting her in every way I could, and still she would nag on and on from the moment I walked into the house late in the evenings, exhausted from work, to the moment I left again at six-thirty in the morning.

'Why are you wearing that? Why are you wearing so much make-up? Why can't you wear something else? Why have you got heels on?'

If I came in and sat in a sofa she would want to know why I was sitting there rather than the chair next to the sewing machine where she was constantly working.

'Why are you sitting there?' she would whine. 'Is my face so ugly that you can't sit and look at me?'

There wasn't a single thing I could do or say that she wouldn't criticise or question.

There was an Indian girl at work who called herself Penny and whom I had become very friendly with. She was completely different to me in many ways, much more Westernised in her dress, confident in short skirts and high heels, her head uncovered and her face fully made up at all times of the day. We used to take our cigarette breaks together whenever we could and I used to tell her all my woes.

'I've decided to apply for a council flat,' I told her one day. 'I can't stand it at home a moment longer.'

'Can I come and share with you?' she joked. 'We could have such a great time. We could have boys back to the flat whenever we wanted.'

'Whoa,' I laughed, 'not so fast. You can do that if you

want, but I don't want anything to do with your fancy men.'

A few weeks later I moved out of the house and into a flat just across the street, with Mum's hurt voice still ringing in my ears.

'What did I do that was so bad that my only daughter turns her back on me?'

I didn't answer. Despite the guilt she was loading on to my shoulders I was looking forward to getting a life of my own at last.

13

The Sharks Circle

I was beginning to become braver with boys, now that Dad had promised me that I could lead a normal Western life if I came home. There was an Asian boy who had come into the sandwich bar each day for his lunch while I was working there and had asked me out a couple of times. Initially I had said no, mainly because I didn't want the complications of a boyfriend after everything I had been through (I was, after all, technically still a married woman), but also because I was a little unsure what a girl was meant to do on a date with a boy and I didn't want to make a fool of myself. Aman was still really the only person I had ever dated in anything like a normal manner. But this boy was determined to get his way and kept on asking, refusing to accept rejection.

He was good-looking and polite and the other girls in the sandwich bar had egged me on to accept, so in the end I gave in for a quiet life as much as anything. We went out a few times, just going for a McDonald's or to the cinema, that sort of thing. Each time we ended up snogging for ages in his car before he dropped me off home, but I had never wanted it to go any further. I was too scared; scared that sex would hurt and scared of the complications within my family if they ever found out I was doing such things. I had only just managed to make my peace with them and I didn't intend to stir up all that anger again if I didn't have to. Because Ali was away in prison so often, and Asif hardly ever bothered come home, the pressure was off me most of the time, especially once I had moved out of Mum and Dad's house and into my little council flat. I didn't want to do anything to reignite all the old battles.

Mum would still get at me whenever I went round to see her, which was most days, but she hardly went anywhere else by that stage, unless it was home to Lahore for visits, so she didn't come to the flat. I think she stayed away partly out of principle, wanting to show me that she didn't accept that I had a home of my own. Dad was hardly ever there when I called round, always working or out with friends, avoiding Mum's nagging, but I knew if I made any more big mistakes the family could easily all turn on me again, and on any boy who dared to disrespect them by sleeping with me.

I made sure I didn't fall in love either because the break-up with Aman had been too painful and there was no way I wanted to go through anything like that again. At the same time I did want to feel close to someone, to have a man be affectionate to me in the way Aman had been when he had kissed me and when we went to bed together, someone who would be as kind and patient, and this boy seemed to be doing all the right things.

'Take your time,' he would say as he caressed and kissed me in the car and I told him I didn't want to go any further. 'There's no rush. Whenever you are ready.'

I didn't tell him, but at that moment I couldn't imagine that I would ever want to have sex again, any more than I wanted to fall in love again. It worried me a bit and I talked to Penny about it, because I had found that I could say anything to her.

'Don't worry,' she reassured me. 'When the time's right you'll be able to do it. You were OK with Aman, weren't you? You just need to meet more boys and relax a bit. Have you ever been clubbing?'

I laughed at the thought of it. 'Me? Clubbing? I don't think I would fit in anywhere like that, do you?'

'Rubbish,' she said. 'Why on earth not? I'm taking you and no arguing.'

'But I don't even know what clothes to wear.'

She ignored all my protests.

'I'll take you shopping!'

She clapped her hands happily at the thought and I found her excitement infectious. Even though the idea of clubs and bars was as frightening as travelling to a new country for me, I had a feeling it was going to be an experience that I would enjoy once I overcame my fears, and at least I would have Penny there to show me what to do.

Now that I was in my own flat I was able to open my own wage packet at the end of the week and just give Mum what I could spare. She had no idea how much I was earning in my new catering job and I was able to hold back enough so that I could go shopping with Penny for an outfit that would suit this new adventure in my life.

The following Saturday we headed to the city centre and Penny led me from one shop to another, leaving me dazed from the music, the lights and the dozens of garments she was waving at me, holding up against me or making me try on in cramped and crowded changing rooms. Once I got over the embarrassment of dressing and undressing among so many people I found I was beginning to enjoy myself. Once or twice I got a glimpse of my reflection in a shop mirror and I actually didn't look too bad compared to the image of myself I had been carrying in my head all my life. We eventually settled on a long, backless dress with a slit up the side and two hooks holding it together at the nape of my neck. I had never worn anything so revealing in my life. It felt as if I was going to be appearing virtually naked in public. It was a frightening feeling, but it was exciting too, in a way I had never experienced before. Without

Penny's encouragement I would never have had the nerve
to buy it.

'You need a strapless bra to go under it,' she told me as
she whisked me from shop to shop, 'and we want some
really good heels to show off your legs.'

'I won't even know how to put these things on,' I
protested. 'Or how to put on make-up properly. I'll look
ridiculous.'

'Don't worry,' she laughed. 'I'll come over and help you
get ready.'

Although Penny hadn't actually moved into the flat with
me, she was there nearly all the time and kept a lot of her
stuff permanently in my spare wardrobe. Using a mixture
of her own make-up and the products that she had made
me buy, she set about transforming me that first Saturday
evening. When I finally viewed the result in the full-length
mirror it was like the final scene in one of those television
makeover programmes. I couldn't believe my eyes. It was
as if I was looking at a different person. Penny had made
me look ten years younger and two stone slimmer. High on
our own excitement, we headed for a pub to meet Penny's
older sister, giggling like two naughty schoolgirls doing
something forbidden, with me struggling to master the art
of walking in high heels and looking as if it was natural.

'My sister has a husband,' Penny had told me, 'but the
spice has gone out of the relationship, if you know what I

mean. She used to have black boyfriends before she got married, so she's used to having a good sex life and now she's not getting it.'

I was shocked by her words, but I wanted to find out more. I couldn't understand how any woman would dare to behave in such a brazen way, making such demands of the men in her life. This was a whole new world that I knew nothing about; the world that the others girls at school had alluded to in their half-informed way, leaving me stranded and speechless in my ignorance. As I watched the men coming into the bar on their own or with other men, laughing and posing and eyeing all the women, it occurred to me that this was also the world that my brothers had been inhabiting when they were away from the family, a parallel life that they never talked about at home. Now I was going to find out for myself what it was all about and what I had been missing out on for so many years. It was my turn to have some fun, if I could just pluck up the courage.

The pub was big and so crowded that customers were spilling out into the street just to find somewhere to stand and drink. We had to push through the crowd to get near the bar and I was surprised when none of the men groped us. It would have been impossible to get through a crowd this dense in Lahore without ending up black and blue from the pinching. If I had been wearing a dress like the one I had on I would have caused a street riot. There was a disc jockey operating in the corner of a dance floor where a number of couples were already strutting their stuff. I felt the adrenaline pumping through my veins to the beat of the music. This was like a different planet to the dreary world of home, where the whirr of Mum's sewing machine was usually the only sound competing with the constant burble of the television with its canned laughter and over-excited chatter. This was the real, live world where people were doing whatever they wanted and enjoying themselves while they were still young and free, without worrying too much about the consequences.

Penny's sister hooked up with a man almost immediately after we got there and disappeared through the crowd and out the back somewhere. It wasn't long before Penny had done the same, leaving me sitting in a corner booth squeezed in among strangers who all seemed to know one another and didn't seem to notice I was there as I waited for one or other of them to come back. I kept my eyes firmly averted from any passing men, not yet feeling brave enough to follow my friends' leads, not even completely sure what it was they had gone off to do. Were they just dancing and snogging? Or were they going further in an alley somewhere or in the backseat of a parked car? In a way I was cross with myself for my own failure of nerve because there were several nice-looking men who had tried to catch my eye, but it was too big a bridge to cross on my first time out in such a place. Even though I hadn't done anything very daring, I was still buzzing with excitement when we eventually went home at the end of the night.

The next day, when she had sobered up, Penny was cross-examining me about what I had got up to while we were separated in the pub. I told her I hadn't done anything, explaining that it didn't matter how good I had felt in the dress and heels, I was still scared of sex, especially with strangers in a pub.

'You don't have to be,' she told me. 'All men aren't like your husband.'

I knew that was true, because of my experience with Aman, but I had already known he was a good, kind and gentle man before I went to bed with him. And I was pretty sure that the man from the sandwich bar had been good and kind, although he had eventually grown tired of waiting and stopped asking me out. But how could I tell the good ones from the bad ones if I was just picking them up in a crowded pub? It was all very confusing. Penny spent the whole week reassuring me, promising that it would all be OK.

'There's plenty more nights,' she said, 'and plenty more clubs. We'll try again.'

In the following weeks I began to realise that I might have been a bit too rash in accepting a council flat. Along with the money that I still felt obliged to give Mum and Dad if I didn't want them to drown in debt, I was now having to find enough to pay my own rent and bills. I confided my problem to Penny.

'I'm going to introduce you to a friend of mine,' she said, taking charge of the situation in her usual way. 'She's really nice and she's got a room to rent in her house. She'll charge you less than half what your flat is costing you.'

Her friend was called Karen, another Indian girl with progressive views, just like Penny. She was really keen for me to move in and the room she was renting was exactly what I needed. She said she would charge me just fifty pounds a week with all the bills included, which sounded like a brilliant deal. Karen was even prettier than Penny, really slim and busty. The first weekend that I was there, as I had taken a couple of days off work to move in, she came into my room for a chat.

'You ever been clubbing?' she asked.

'Not really,' I admitted. 'I went to a pub with a dance floor with Penny a few weeks ago, but that's all.'

'Let's go out together tonight then,' she suggested. 'I'll show you some good places.'

Although I had been too nervous to talk to any of the men, I had enjoyed my night out with Penny and I did want to have another go. The boy from the sandwich shop seemed to have finally given up any hope of our relationship going anywhere and I didn't fancy a Saturday night in a bedsit on my own, any more than I fancied going round to Mum's and listening to her complaining endlessly about Dad. I wanted to meet new people and try to have a bit of fun. I didn't get so dressed up this time, just putting on some trousers and a T-shirt, so I didn't feel quite as conspicuous, and Karen took me to a really nice club where everyone seemed to know her and she was able to introduce me around and make me feel at home. It wasn't nearly as crowded as the pub had been, with plenty of places to sit and talk. I had a few dances with men Karen introduced me to and I drank alcohol for the first time when she bought me an Archers and lemonade. My inhibitions slowly melted in the warm, friendly atmosphere as the drink seeped through me. By the end of the night I went home feeling more confident and good about myself than I had ever felt in my whole life. One or two of the men had asked if I would like to go home with them, but I didn't yet feel ready to cross that barrier, even though Karen ended up bringing home a guy in a very expensive-looking car.

After that it became a regular outing for us on any weekend night that I wasn't working, and I noticed that Karen always seemed to end up with a different man at the end of the night, all of whom would give her a lift home in their smart cars and would then stay the night. The funny thing was that none of these men seemed to become regular boyfriends. There was a new one virtually every time and they always left first thing the following morning, which didn't seem to bother Karen in the least.

By the second or third visit to the club I was feeling comfortable enough to be willing to chat to anyone, even complete strangers who came up and introduced themselves. As the weeks went by I noticed that a lot of the customers were regulars, always there every time I went. Eventually I met a man who I really liked and grew to trust enough to let him gently and determinedly take me home to bed. Despite having had a good few drinks I was still terrified, but at the same time I really wanted to get over my fear. I didn't want to think that my short fling with Aman was going to be the only love I would ever experience. All the other girls I was now socialising with seemed to be enjoying sex without any hang-ups at all and I didn't want to spend the next ten years worrying about it and missing out on all the fun. I explained to my new friend that I'd had bad experiences and he was as patient and careful with me as Aman had been.

The sex wasn't as good as it had been with Aman because I didn't have the same strong feelings, but it was good enough for me to think that I would like to do it again. It hadn't been painful and it had been fun and irresponsible, different to everything that had ever happened to me before. All my life everything had been so serious and so loaded with consequences that it felt wonderful to simply be self-indulgent for a few hours. I had expected that I would feel guilty for having sex outside marriage, given how I'd had those messages drummed into me virtually from the day I was born, but it didn't feel like that. It just felt like a new and interesting life experience. Everyone I was mixing with took it all so naturally, without any worry or anxiety and, away from the influence of my family, I fell into the same pattern of thinking.

I was working so hard to make enough money to give Mum and Dad that I didn't have that much spare time for my newly discovered social life, but probably every two or three months I would take someone back home, happy to say goodbye to them the following morning just like Karen did, not wanting any more from them than that. I certainly didn't feel that I wanted to start a long-term relationship with any of them. I'd had enough of men telling me what to do to last me a lifetime, I just wanted to have some fun now and then, to feel in charge of my own destiny. There were probably only four or five different guys in all over the next eighteen months, one or two of whom I saw several times. Compared to Karen and Penny it wasn't that many at all, but it seemed like a lot to me. They were all nice guys and they helped to rebuild my confidence still further by treating me respectfully and paying me lots of compliments. To begin with, for instance, I had wanted to have the light turned out, not wanting them to see my naked body, believing I was fat and ugly and dirty-looking like Mum had always told me. Gradually they convinced me that I was attractive, that I could leave the light on and feel proud of my body, that the colour of my skin was one of the things that had attracted them to me in the first place. It was a wonderful revelation to me to think that I might actually be attractive after all.

My divorce from Ahmed went through as a matter of course, aided by his statement to the embassy that he had only married me in order to get a visa. Although I had always felt that the marriage had been unlawful because of the speed with which it was conducted, it was still a relief to know that I was officially divorced and no longer had to think that I was being unfaithful to my husband. I was able to tell myself that I was a single girl again and could do as I pleased.

Now that I felt more confident and independent I didn't mind going back home for visits so much. Mum hadn't changed, but I could put up with the complaining and the nagging if I knew I was only going to be there for a few hours and that I could get back to my own room whenever I felt like it. Dad seemed to be at home more often than he used to be, maybe because there was only him and Mum there most of the time, as my sister-in-law tended to go back to her mother's whenever Ali was in prison. He didn't appear to feel the need to escape as often, or maybe he was just growing older and losing the urge to wander.

The subject that always seemed to be at the front of both their minds was money. Their debts were growing much worse, and yet they were still sending money back to Lahore or giving it to my sisters-in-law to help with the costs of bringing up their grandchildren whenever Ali was in jail or Asif had disappeared on one of his mysterious trips. Mum had started to confide in me things that I knew she wasn't even telling Dad. It didn't matter how little money Mum had, she would always send the bulk of it back to her brothers and sisters. Even after so many years she still felt that they were her primary responsibility, still putting them before her own children. I suppose I was now doing the same, making my own life hard in order to make sure my parents had the money they needed, even though I didn't think they should be giving so much of it away. I did want to make life more comfortable for my mum and dad, I wanted to pay their bills and put food on their table, but I resented providing money to be sent back to an endless stream of uncles and aunts and cousins in Pakistan, many of whom I barely even knew.

Without telling Dad, Mum had borrowed a few thousand from a loan shark to send back for a family funeral, but the interest she was being charged had multiplied the debt out of all proportion. It had started with her talking to some women she was friendly with at the local corner shop. She had told them how desperate she was for money and they, in their ignorance, had told her of people they knew who would be willing to lend it to her. The sharks would charge fifty per cent interest a week on everything she owed. So, if she borrowed a thousand pounds, she owed £1,500 by the end of the first week, £2,250 by the end of the second and so on. The sharks would even add extra penalty charges for late payment. Eventually Dad had to be told because the creditors were starting to come round the house demanding payment. Dad was furious with her for getting into so much debt without telling him, but he knew they had to pay up. The sharks persuaded Mum and Dad to sign away the deeds to their house, so then there was a danger that if they didn't keep up the payments their home would be taken away from them to settle the debt. They were living in fear, but the sums they needed were beyond anything I could possibly hope to give them in one go. All I could do was give them a little bit at a time to keep the sharks at bay at least.

I was working incredibly long days and because my rent was so low I was able to give them a fair bit of money each week, but it was still never enough to get rid of the basic debts, which kept on mounting up. Every time I came home Mum seemed to have taken out another loan, always claiming that this was money they had to have in order to help this relative with a marriage or that one with a new baby. I began to realise, however, that a lot of the creditors coming to the house were people that Ali owed money to for drug deals that had gone wrong. It seemed that over the years he had been using merchandise that he should have been dealing, which meant he had no money to pay his suppliers. Drug dealers are frightening people to owe money to.

In the past Dad had always been very against borrowing money from anyone outside the family, but he didn't seem to be able to stop Mum any more. It was as if he was giving up the fight. I felt angry inside at the way they were handling their affairs, but I couldn't show it because that would have been disrespectful and would have gone against everything I had ever been taught as a child. It would also have looked as if I didn't want to give them the money and was trying to find excuses to get out of my duties to them.

The debt collectors were growing more threatening with every visit and once or twice I took the money directly to them myself, to make sure that it got to them and wasn't diverted to Asif's pocket, or Ali in jail or to some other needy relative in Lahore. They were frightening, foul-mouthed, violent men and I could see how they were able to intimidate Mum into paying them more and more with their threats. In a way she had become their slave now, just as she had once been the family's slave, doing as much piecework as she could to scrape together enough money to satisfy their latest demands. But it didn't matter how hard she worked because she was only being paid five pence for every skirt or pair of jeans she sewed, so it was impossible for her to make anything like enough money to match their escalating demands, there simply weren't enough hours in the day.

I had been living with Karen for nearly two years when my boss came to see me at a venue where I was managing a job for him. I was up to my eyes in work, overseeing the needs of about a hundred guests and not able to pay him that much attention, but I could see that he was looking serious. When there was finally time for me to take a break he steered me outside with a coffee.

'You are a good worker, Saira,' he told me, 'one of the best I've ever had, but there have been problems with the business.'

'What do you mean, problems?' I felt a sinking feeling in my stomach. This reminded me of the grown-up talks I had overheard when our own family business had fallen apart and Dad had had to go and work at the petrol station just to have enough money coming in to support us.

'It is a family business,' he went on, obviously embarrassed, 'and I have other family members that I have to give jobs to. I can't afford to keep on everyone, I'm sorry.'

'You're firing me?' I couldn't get my head round what he was saying. I had thought he was taking me aside to tell me how well I was doing, maybe even to offer me a rise.

'I could offer you work as a waitress,' he said, trying to make that sound like a solution, 'but not as a manager.'

I knew how much the waitresses were paid and it wasn't enough to even come close to paying the interest on Mum's loans, let alone all the other expenses we had to meet each month.

'I need this job,' I said, weakly. 'I have a lot of problems.'

'I will give you a good reference,' he said, looking as if he wanted the ground to open up and swallow him.

Getting another job wasn't going to be a problem, but getting one that allowed me to earn as much as I had been making with him was almost impossible. I had no qualifications that I could show anyone and employers all seemed to want to hire people with degrees or training. Several companies offered to take me on as a waitress, suggesting that I would be able to 'work my way back up', but I didn't think I had time to start all over again. I couldn't imagine the loan sharks were going to be very impressed with me telling them I'd had a salary cut and wouldn't be able to meet their payments quite as soon as I had hoped. I went back to a local garment factory initially, just because that was a world I knew and where I could start work immediately, but they would have taken me on whether I had a glowing reference or not. All they cared about was that I could sew fast in a straight line for hours on end. I had bought myself a car while I was earning well. I was paying it off monthly, which was another drain on my resources, but because I still owed a lot on it I wouldn't have realised any money by selling it. There had to be another way round the problem, I was sure of it. I was determined to keep my room and my independence and not go back to living at home. I thought Mum and I might well kill each other if we were forced to live under the same roof all the time again.

Karen could see what was happening because I no longer had the energy or the money to go out clubbing at weekends.

'You can't go on like this forever,' she told me one night when I came in from work at nearly midnight, looking half dead with exhaustion. 'You should go and see this clairvoyant I use, she's really good. She'll tell you what's in store for you so you can stop worrying and maybe stop working your fingers to the bone.'

Initially I resisted because I thought it was a waste of money, but then one day I had some time off and I decided to treat myself. What I didn't realise was that by making that simple, seemingly frivolous decision I was about to change everything.

14

The Escort Business

The clairvoyant was an older woman, very down-to-earth and easy to talk to. What I really hoped she was going to tell me was whether I would be coming into any money in the near future that would help me out with all my troubles. She told me quite a bit about myself, but nothing that really helped me out with my decisions as to what to do with my life. We got into a conversation after she had given me my reading, as she had a very relaxed and under-standing manner. I found myself telling her all my woes, most of which centred around money. I had been racking my brains for ideas about how to earn enough to get my parents out of trouble while also keeping my independence and I had heard several people talking about 'escort work'. I had seen some advertisements for girls interested in the work in the local papers, but without really understanding what it was. I hadn't liked to ask my friends for fear of appearing stupid. I had been mocked often enough when I was at school for my lack of worldly knowledge but I somehow felt I could ask this woman anything.

'What is escort work exactly?' I enquired innocently.

'It probably isn't quite what you think,' she smiled kindly. 'It doesn't mean just going out to dinner with men, you know.'

'What does it mean then?' I asked, genuinely puzzled.

'It means sleeping with the clients,' she said. 'Hasn't Karen explained it to you?'

That was the moment when all the pieces of the jigsaw fell into place in my head. That explained all those different men coming back to the house in their smart cars, and it explained why Karen always had plenty of money to spend on clothes and anything else she wanted and how she came to own her own house when she was still so young. I sat for a moment, taking this revelation in.

'Actually,' the clairvoyant went on cheerfully, 'you'd probably do really, really well at it.'

'Why?' I asked, surprised and not sure whether to be flattered or insulted. I had always assumed that I was a plain girl; surely anyone earning their living this way would need to be beautiful like Karen.

'Because you're Indian,' she said, and I didn't bother to correct her. I often found it was easier to let people who didn't know my family think I was from India rather than Pakistan. There always seemed to be a lot less prejudice towards Indians and there wasn't the whole Muslim thing. 'There's a big demand out there for Indian girls. Lots of

men really love dark skins. And there are your other assets.'
She glanced down at my breasts. 'You'd make a killing.'

'Do you really think so?'

It was the first time I had heard that Indian girls were
considered desirable and it surprised me after everything
Mum had always said to me about my dark skin and how
unattractive it was. I had always assumed men preferred the
Western girls, with their pale skins and revealing clothes,
but over the following years I found out that the clairvoyant
was right. One white client explained to me later how he
had lived for years in an area where there were lots of Asian
families and all the women covered themselves up most of
the time.

'When you're sitting opposite a young woman who is all
covered, or you see one in the street,' he explained, 'your
mind does wander. You do wonder what she would look
like without clothes and what it would be like to sleep with
her.'

By forcing their women to cover up, Asian men had
actually made them more attractive to other men, exactly
the opposite of the result they wanted to achieve.

'You mean I would have to have sex with strange men?'
I asked the clairvoyant, still trying to get my head round the
idea.

'Well, you give it away for a bunch of roses and a box of
chocolates anyway, don't you?' she laughed.

'Yes,' I grinned sheepishly, 'I suppose so.'

'So, why not get paid for it?'

We changed the subject after that and I don't suppose she thought anything more about it, but I kept finding myself going over the conversation in my head during the next few days as I laboured over my sewing machine, and the more I thought about it the more I began to see the sense in what she had said. All the one-night-stands I'd indulged in had been OK up to a point, and I had enjoyed being an object of desire to them even if it was only at a shallow level. None of them had been as bad as the agony I'd had to endure with Ahmed. They had taught me to be less afraid of men and shown me that I could assert myself if I needed to, that I did not have to be a doormat like my mother just because I was a woman. Would it have been any different if they had paid me, I wondered? Imagine if I had been paid for all the times Ahmed had raped me; I would have been a rich woman by the time I left him.

Now that I had found out what Karen was doing for a living I looked around and I realised a lot of the girls that I had been socialising with in the clubs must have been doing the same. It was as if the scales had been lifted from my eyes. Was I the only one who had been giving it away for free? They all seemed to be having just as good a time as me. None of them seemed to fit the stereotype of a prostitute that I had always carried around in my head. They didn't look like the women I'd sometimes seen lurking around in the dark streets behind the station, most of whom looked as if they were out of their heads on drugs, their arms and chests covered in tattoos, and their young faces spoiled by sores. My friends in the clubs were just normal girls who were willing to have sex with men, none of them particularly glamorous or special, just nice-looking. I realised I was seriously considering doing the same myself. It seemed as if it might be fun.

That Sunday I had a day off and I went round to see Mum and Dad. Dad was out and the debt collectors were outside the front of the house, shouting abuse and threats through the windows and banging on the door. When they saw me coming they turned their attention to me, knowing I was the one who had come up with the money in the past. Other people in neighbouring houses must have been able to hear the noise the men were making, but no one came out to see if I was all right. One of the men snatched my bag off my shoulder and emptied the contents on to the ground. Scooping up my purse, he took the few pounds I had left and thrust his face into mine, his fingers squeezing painfully into my neck.

'You're not keeping up with the payments,' he hissed. 'You need to come and see us every week or your mum and dad may end up having to look for somewhere else to live. Do you understand?'

I nodded, unable to find the breath to speak, not wanting to make them any angrier than they already were. They pushed me to the ground among my scattered possessions and sauntered back to their car. I pulled myself up and quickly scooped my things back into my bag. I was still shaking when I finally persuaded Mum it was safe to open the door and let me in. I knew then that I was going to have to do something radical if I was ever going to get these people off our backs. It almost seemed that it was a sign, sent to help me make my mind up. The next day I summoned all my courage and rang one of the escort agencies that advertised in the paper.

'I've never done anything like this before,' I said when they answered, 'but are you looking for girls?'

The woman's voice at the other end of the phone sounded much friendlier than I had expected and she asked me how old I was, what race and what dress size. I confessed I was about a size twelve or fourteen, thinking she would probably end the conversation right there, but she said that would be fine. She gave me an address to come to that evening. I took care dressing myself and putting on my make-up as if I was going to the club, wanting to make myself look as attractive as possible. I squirted myself liberally with Christian Dior's Poison before leaving the house. I loved my perfumes, maybe because of all the years when people had told me at school that I had body odour.

The address she had given me turned out to be a rough-looking council block in an area I wouldn't normally have wanted to be walking around on my own at night. The concrete stairwells stank of urine and the walkways to the front doors of the flats were littered with old rubbish that people had thrown out and no one had cleared away. When I found the front door I wanted I could see it had obviously been broken into and reinforced afterwards. The windows had an elaborate network of bars on them too. My heart was thumping as I tapped shyly on the door, keen to get safely inside before anyone else appeared on the walkway. I could hear ugly voices shouting from round a corner somewhere, as if someone was having a major domestic argument and didn't care who knew about it.

The woman who opened the door was the same one I had spoken to on the phone. She was bigger and more frightening-looking than I had been imagining from her voice, but still seemed perfectly friendly to me. She didn't look attractive enough to have been on the game herself, but it was possible she had just let herself go. She led me through into a sitting room. The inside of the flat was like a different world to the graffiti-smeared grey concrete outside. It looked as if no expense had been spared on the marbled floors and cream-coloured furnishings. There were four or more phones dotted around the room, which I later discovered were all linked to a variety of numbers that were being advertised around town as different agencies, one specialising in black girls, another offering girls with big breasts and so forth. It seemed this was a market made up of many specialised niches. Four girls were sitting around on the sofas, all of them dolled up as if they were waiting to go out on dates. I noticed that none of them were Indian and all of them looked a lot slimmer and prettier than I believed I was, although their expressions looked hard and bitchy as they eyed me up and down. I wondered if I was making a mistake and would be sent away for not being attractive or slim enough.

'She's wearing too much perfume,' one of them said as I walked past, but the woman in charge didn't take any notice as she led me through to a state-of-the-art kitchen that looked as if it had just been installed and didn't get used that often. Getting out a notebook and tape measure she checked my statistics and noted them down without showing any sign of doubts or disapproval. I felt my confidence climbing a few notches up the scale.

'It's three hundred pounds an hour,' she said as she worked, 'a hundred and fifty for half an hour. For half an hour you get to keep ninety pounds for yourself, for an hour you get to keep a hundred and thirty.'

'OK.' I didn't know what else to say. I assumed this meant she was agreeing to take me on. In a way I was relieved, but there was part of me that had been hoping I would be turned down and allowed to scurry back to the safety of my own room, able to tell myself that I had tried my best but was just too ugly to be an escort.

'Let me make a couple of phone calls for you,' she said once she had finished with the measuring. 'Maybe I can get you a client for this evening.'

I hadn't expected things to move so fast, but I didn't dare protest or ask for more time to think about things. I didn't think this woman would appreciate having her time wasted and I was pretty sure the girls in the other room would enjoy being given permission to give someone a good kicking. She dialled a number and didn't bother to announce who she was before speaking.

'I've got somebody fresh for you,' she said, staring at me as she spoke. 'She's never done it before. She's Indian, dark-skinned, busty, all natural, black hair.'

All my life I had been told that I was dirty and ugly-looking because of the darkness of my skin and because I wasn't skinny, and now I was hearing these features being described as assets. Despite feeling nervous in such alien surroundings I experienced a little glow of pride at the thought that this woman actually thought there were men who would be willing to pay for what I had to offer.

The man on the other end of the line must have told her to send me down to see him.

'OK,' she said, hanging up the phone. 'Go to this address.' She scribbled a name and address down on a scrap of paper. 'Come back here with my money as soon as you've finished.'

'Is there anything else I should know?' I asked.

'Always get the money up front.' She thought for a second. 'Be careful the clients don't slip anything into your drinks and when you get to a location check all the doors and cupboards to make sure no one is filming. But this guy is a regular client so you won't have any trouble.'

She gave me some rough directions on how to find the address and sent me back out past the other girls, who I guess must have been fed up that I was being given a job so quickly while they were still sitting around waiting.

I still had my car, which was another reason why I needed money so desperately as I was already falling behind with the payments, but I needed it that night as the address turned out to be a large factory on the outskirts of town producing some sort of heavy-duty steelwork. A taxi ride all that way would have cost me a fortune, which I didn't imagine the escort lady would be willing to refund. It was dark by the time I found the factory and the night shift was already at work. As well as being frightened I felt exhausted, which probably helped to dull the fear a bit.

This was the night when I was given one more chance to turn back from the course I had chosen. My first client was the factory manager who sent me away because I was wearing too much perfume. The experience had certainly been more frightening than I had expected and the moment I was back in my car I locked the doors and sped away as quickly as possible to pay the woman at the agency and get back to the safety of my own home. I couldn't believe what a narrow escape I'd had. Part of me was relieved to have come away unharmed, but beneath that superficial relief lay a deep, dark pool of dread at the thought of how many more places like that factory I might be going to have to visit, and how differently things might turn out next time; the thought made me feel physically sick and I had to push it out of my mind, reminding myself of the three hundred pounds that had been so easily earned.

The woman took her share of the money without even bothering to count it. 'Next time don't wear so much perfume,' was all she said. There were still other girls sitting around the lounge area making bitchy comments as I passed, but I didn't take any notice. I was too tired to care about anything by then, I just wanted to get home to my bed.

She rang again the next evening with another job. Having had time to calm down after the previous night I had realised that it had been incredibly easy money. I liked the idea of earning another hundred and thirty pounds before I had finished the day. When someone was actually offering me a job that would pay so much cash so quickly I found it impossible to resist. I kept telling myself how much it would help with the payments to Mum's creditors and how the ordeal would all be over in a few hours.

This time the address she gave me turned out to be a private house which had been divided up into a couple of flats, and the door was opened by a much younger guy than the night before, wearing nothing but a bathrobe. I could tell he had been drinking, which was a little scary, but he was still a nice-looking man and the house had a cosy, unthreatening feel to it. He offered me a drink once I was sitting down, which I accepted, watching carefully as he poured it to make sure he didn't slip anything into it. Then we sat and chatted for a while and he told me that he had just broken up with his girlfriend and was feeling a bit lonely.

'This is the first time I've done anything like this,' he said.

'You mean you've never hired an escort before?'

'No,' he grinned sheepishly.

'I've never done it before either,' I said, telling him about my aborted adventure the previous night.

By the time we finally went through to the bedroom it

felt more like a normal one-night-stand than a professional engagement. I could feel my heartbeat quickening at the sight of the bed, so neatly made and turned down to wait for us. As he pulled me close to him it felt unnatural and too soon to be that close, but I knew I couldn't pull back as my instincts told me to because this was what I was being paid for. I had been to bed with enough men by then to know how to go through the motions, a bit like an actress.

He had taken the trouble of showering and applying aftershave before I got there so he smelled nice and clean as he pressed himself against me. To my surprise I found myself becoming aroused as he slid my clothes off, dropped his robe to the floor and guided me down on to the bed. He was caressing and kissing me so gently I didn't feel in the least afraid, just puzzled as to what he was planning to do as he slid right down beneath the sheets and parted my thighs. When I realised he was actually going to give me oral sex, I was shocked. I didn't even know men did those sorts of things. Certainly no man had ever done that for me before, not even Aman. For a second I was embarrassed to think he would do such a thing, worried that he would think I smelled bad, but within a few moments I couldn't believe how good it felt to have his tongue and lips playing with me rhythmically. I was twenty-five years old by then and had never been given an orgasm before by anyone. It was a revelation that anyone would care enough to want to do something so wonderful for me, particularly a man who was a virtual stranger and had paid for the privilege to do whatever he wanted.

I think perhaps if that night had gone badly I might have given up the whole idea of being an escort, but I actually walked out to my car later floating on air. The sex I had been having with the various one-night-stands had been OK, but compared to what had just happened I could now see that it had all been unsatisfying and a bit boring. I hadn't realised how much frustration had been building up inside me until that guy released it all. I left his flat knowing I definitely wanted more of that. If even ten per cent of my future clients were going to make me feel like that, I reasoned, then escort work was not going to be such a bad way to earn a living after all.

I sometimes wonder what would have happened if seeing that client had turned out to be a bad experience. Would I have given up then? Maybe it would have been better if he hadn't been such a nice, kind and generous man. But at the same time I will always be grateful to him for giving me that tiny glimpse into what was possible.

15

Becoming a Professional

After that first job the work began to fall into a more predictable pattern. Mostly it was boring, sometimes it was faintly disgusting, occasionally it was fun and occasionally it was frightening.

Most of the time I would be sent to one or two clients a week, the majority of whom were businessmen staying in nice hotels. Nine times out of ten the guys were OK-looking and reasonably considerate about my feelings, although none of them was ever as good in bed as that first guy in the bathrobe. Now and then I would come across an unpleasant one, who would treat me as if I wasn't a person at all, which would remind me just how haram the whole business was, but it was never bad enough to frighten me off. The money more than made up for the disadvantages.

The Asian men were nearly always the most chauvinistic and unpleasant clients. I suppose they automatically looked down on anyone who did this kind of work, even though I could only do it because men like them were willing to pay me. Perhaps there was an element of self-hatred contributing to their bitterness as well. I know that many of them would have beaten and maybe even killed the women in their families if they had ever caught them doing what I was doing. It was as if they felt they had to dominate any woman they were with in order to show they were real men and to demonstrate their contempt for us. They gave no thought to how I might be feeling and saw nothing wrong with treating me badly. As far as they were concerned I was less than human.

British men were always much more considerate and respectful, treating me as a person rather than a piece of dirt, often wanting to please me before they took their own pleasure. Very few of them were able to do that, of course, but I didn't let them know it. But the Asian ones would just want me to demean myself, leaving me on my knees pleasuring them orally for the whole time I was with them just so they could look down on me and insult me.

Over the following years the one or two clients a week would eventually build up to several clients a day and sometimes it would be hard to keep going and to psyche myself up to go through the whole charade over and over again, but the constant and increasing need for money drove me on. I would always have a target figure in my head, a sum that I knew I had to make that day in order to pay Mum's latest bill or debt, and I would keep on working till I had made that sum, seeing client after client after client, closing my mind to everything else around me until I knew I had earned enough money to be able to relax until the next day.

No matter how hard I worked, however, or how much money I gave them, things just kept on getting worse at home. Dad would never ask me for money, but Mum would keep me informed of every tiny detail of their deepening financial ruin on a daily basis. If they weren't going to be able to meet the mortgage repayments that month she would make sure I knew, if there was a death in the family or a marriage she would let me know that they couldn't afford to do what was necessary and I would understand that she expected me to find the money. If Ali came round to see her with a dealer that he owed money to she would let me know exactly how much the debt was and how terrible it was for him to be so embarrassed. If the debt collectors came round with their threats she would be sobbing down the phone and my heart would feel as if it was going to break on her behalf, even though I would be feeling angry with her at the same time for allowing herself to fall into such an obvious trap. Knowing as I did what her childhood and early adulthood had been like, I could understand how much of an innocent she must have been about life in Britain and how she had never really been able to bridge the gap between the two cultures, making her an easy catch for these ruthless predators.

Now that she no longer saw my pay packets each week

she had no idea how much or little I earned, she just knew that whenever she asked me I would step forward and try to pay for what was needed. Sometimes, after she had been talking to some other relative who had been dishing out advice without understanding the full situation she would become annoyed that I wasn't paying the loan sharks off completely. I would try to explain how I wasn't earning enough to meet the interest payments, but I don't think she really understood. My father never knew the full extent of the money she was taking from me so I never had to explain to him how I managed to earn so much so quickly.

Occasionally I would get annoyed by her nagging and I would lose my temper and grumble at her. She would then sulk for a few days, and the next time she needed money she would go to another member of the family for yet another loan rather than humbling herself by asking me. She would then find herself unable to pay it back yet again and would have to come back to me once more to confess what she had done.

'Why didn't you tell me you needed this money?' I would ask each time.

'I didn't want to burden you,' she would always reply, as if she was the one taking all the burden on to her own shoulders.

So I could never really complain when she did tell me all her woes because I needed to know what was going on, and

I couldn't turn my back on her when she needed my help because I knew it was my duty as a daughter to support her and my father in any way I could.

It didn't take long for me to start behaving like a seasoned professional when it came to dealing with clients. There were certain things I wouldn't do for them, like anal sex or anything without a condom, but within the range that I was comfortable with I would try to give them good value for money and I would always treat them with the sort of politeness and respect I wanted them to show towards me. When I started out I knew nothing about any different varieties of sex, but I picked things up quickly as I went along. I knew in theory what blowjobs were for instance, but had never done one and wasn't sure exactly how to go about it. One of the first clients I went to in a hotel, however, was watching a blue film when I got there (I hadn't even realised you could do something like that in a hotel room), and the actors were performing oral sex in that, so I watched carefully and saw what was done. It didn't look that pleasant but I thought I could probably do it as long as the men were wearing condoms. In fact it usually wasn't too difficult because the customers would almost always come the moment I got them in my mouth, so I hardly ever had to do it for more than a few seconds.

Even for that short a time, however, the taste and smell

was disgusting. I doubt I will ever be able to forget the unpleasant rubbery tang of condoms, but that was still better than doing it without protection. Even the cleanest men smell dirty and musty when they whip their underpants down and I always found it a job not to gag as I went down on them, trying to avoid breathing through my nose for as long as possible. It doesn't matter what flavour the condom manufacturers will tell you they have invented to disguise the taste of rubber, it never works. When they are subjected to friction there is nothing that will cover the stench of hot rubber and I would be able to smell it on my hands or between my legs when I went to the toilet long after the men had gone and I had showered and bathed. Some men would be willing to wash themselves before sex but most weren't willing to put themselves out even that much for a prostitute and I would know it usually was going to be pointless to ask, so I didn't bother.

After a few months I noticed that the agency was getting me fewer bookings and the ones I was getting were at odd times of the night, which made me think they were the ones all the boss's other girls had turned down already. Instead of the nice hotels I had been to previously, I seemed to be being sent to strange places like cottages in the middle of nowhere, which could seem threatening and dangerous at two or three in the morning. Once the agency boss even sent me to a building site, where a man was staying over while he built himself a house. When I plucked up the courage to ask the boss why I didn't seem to be making as much money as I had at the start she just shrugged and said that her regular clients were always looking for something new and different. She didn't seem that interested, as if I had already outlived my usefulness to her and had simply become one more girl among many that she could call on if necessary.

'I need to earn more than this though,' I said. 'Is there anywhere else I might try, where I might be able to get more clients?'

'A lot of the girls work in flats around the city,' she suggested. 'You could try ringing round some of them, see if they need someone like you.'

'Where do I find out about them?' I thought this sounded like something I might be able to do.

'Get the local paper and look in the "personal services" pages,' she said, obviously not bothered at the thought of me working for someone else as well as her. 'They sometimes advertise for staff there.'

I immediately went out and bought a paper and discovered she was right, it had pages full of ads that I had never even noticed in all the years that I had seen Dad reading it around the house. I wondered if he had ever noticed or, if he had, whether he had any idea what the ads were actually for. It seemed there was a big market out there for girls who were willing to do the things that I was now experienced at. I rang one of the numbers and the woman who picked up the phone asked if I would like to go in for an interview. When I got there I was expecting it to be in a rough area like the escort agency, but I was pleasantly surprised. It was a nice flat in a good area, with a cheerful receptionist working in the lounge. The landlady who owned it was a perfectly normal middle-aged woman who you wouldn't give a second glance to in the street. We talked for a while as if this was any normal flat-rental arrangement and she agreed to take me on. The first stage was for an ad to be placed in the paper, in among the dozens like it, describing me as a 'busty Indian girl' and giving the number of the phone in the flat. The receptionist would then handle all the calls and bookings on my behalf and all I had to do was turn up and work in the bedroom in the hours I was booked for.

Working in the flat felt much less frightening than going on my own to places that were miles from anywhere, where anyone could have been waiting to pounce on me from the shadows. If something had gone wrong on any of the escort dates I wouldn't have had anyone there to help me, whereas in the flat I had the receptionist in the room next door all the time, which changed the whole balance of power between me and the clients. Now they were coming to my territory, not the other way round, and I noticed that many of them were quite nervous about it, especially if they were coming for the first time. The prices there were sixty pounds for half an hour, which could include straight or oral sex with a condom. An hour would be a hundred and twenty. I had to pay a third of that money to the woman who owned the flat and I had to pay the receptionist each week as well. I soon worked out that if I had six clients in during the day for half an hour each I would earn three hundred and sixty pounds in total. A hundred and twenty of that would go to the flat owner and I would give the receptionist fifty pounds, leaving me with a hundred and ninety. If the receptionist brought in more than eight clients in any one day she would get an extra fiver per client and I would be able to keep the balance.

Remembering back to my experiences in my marriage, I made sure I used loads of lubrication for penetration so I didn't get too sore and tried to spend as much of the time as possible on foreplay and massages, with some quick sex to finish off at the end. Quite often the client would be so excited to be there at all he would come before he was even inside me. It was very different to having Ahmed rubbing away for hours on end trying to achieve satisfaction over and over again.

Unlike the first time with the man in the bathrobe, which had felt more like a one-night-stand than a professional engagement, I soon learned not to switch my emotions on at all when I was working. I performed like a robot, able to make all the right moves on automatic pilot, thinking all the time about the money I had just taken and how much more I would need to make that day in order to reach whatever my target was. The clients never noticed the difference, they were happy just to be there and to end up having orgasms. If I smiled at them and treated them with the same respect I wanted them to show to me they usually seemed incredibly grateful.

The whole business was driven by the customers' quests for novelty. The woman at the escort agency had been right. Men, I discovered, constantly wanted to find new girls to fuel their fantasies. They would come a few times and then they would grow bored and go off in search of something new and different, and maybe more extreme. Within a few weeks I discovered that I needed to work in several different flats simultaneously in order to keep new customers coming in all the time. There was always a rush of interest at the beginning of each new venture, and then it would peter away after a few months as the customers went in search of new thrills, leaving me with a few regulars at each address.

However many clients I got to meet, however, I always remained essentially mystified by what most of them got from coming to see me, apart from the obvious few seconds of relief. Some of them would be office workers, popping out for a quickie during their lunch hours. They would tell me they had felt so horny all morning they knew they had to do something about it, and then they'd decided they had to come and see me. These were usually ordinary men earning ordinary wages and I couldn't understand how they could manage to justify spending sixty pounds for a half hour with me, especially when the relief they received would probably only last them a few hours before they started wanting it again. Most of them would freely admit that they had wives and girlfriends, so why weren't they having sex with them? Were all these women saying no to their partners? There was one man who dashed in one day saying he had to be quick because he needed to get to the airport and catch a plane.

'Just give me a hand job,' he said. 'I haven't got time for anything else.'

So I gave him what he asked for and he dashed straight off again without even taking his clothes off. Wouldn't it have been easier to go into a toilet somewhere and do it for himself? Another man was holding a conference in a room at the airport. The meeting had finished, but the room was booked for a few more hours so he called the escort agency and asked to have a girl sent over to make use of the room. When I got there he wanted to do it on the table that he had been sitting round with colleagues an hour earlier, discussing God knows what. It was all over very quickly and I couldn't imagine why he thought it would be a thrilling thing to do.

Sometimes men would come to me in the flats after they had been working at sea for a few months, wanting to relieve themselves before they went home to their partners. They would only have had to wait a few more hours and they would have got it for free, then they could have spent the money on buying a nice present for their partners, or on taking them out on a romantic date, which would have ensured they got much better value for their money than they got in that half hour with me. They were willing to take the risk of catching something or of being ripped off, all for the possibility of a few minutes' pleasure with a stranger.

The whole thing was a mystery to me, but it was also my living, so I was hardly going to put any time into trying to persuade them all of the error of their ways. I was there to provide them with whatever they asked for. If I had talked to them honestly they'd only have taken their business to a competitor anyway, they certainly wouldn't have changed their habits or adjusted whatever fantasies they kept in their heads just because I suggested they should.

Some of the clients became regulars, which was nice in a way, but also a potential problem if they became too attached and needed to feel they were friends or lovers rather than paying customers. The chat-up lines they came up with were so predictable it was hard sometimes to keep up the pretence of listening. The first few times that clients told me I was beautiful I felt really flattered, but after a bit I stopped believing them. I realised that no one had ever told me I was beautiful before, so why were they doing it now? It was just because they wanted me to be part of their fantasies. I was only beautiful in their eyes because they needed me to be in order to make themselves feel good about what they were doing. The compliments became meaningless.

'If I had enough money I would take you away from all this,' was another line I heard a lot. They had probably all watched *Pretty Woman* and fancied themselves as the hero. They were all about as much like Richard Gere as I was like Julia Roberts. There were plenty of other women out there, usually in the men's own homes, who they could have gone out with if that was what they wanted. They didn't really want to 'take me away from all this' because then the fantasy would have been over and I would have been just like the wives and partners they were cheating on. Realising this, I never took any of their promises seriously, knowing that they only meant them until they had walked back outside the door into their daily lives.

In my search for other ways to sell my new-found skills,

I also worked for a while in a sauna where there were several other girls. It was based in a house with a reception room downstairs and differently themed bedrooms upstairs. There were Jacuzzis in the rooms and between five and ten girls working there at any one time. I felt a bit of an outsider during the hours when I wasn't with clients and we were all sitting around talking. They all seemed to have been on the game for years and knew all about one another and about all the local pimps, their conversations loaded with references to people I didn't know anything about. They often seemed to come from families where their mothers and aunts and sisters were all in the same business. They were mostly loud and coarse and bitchy and I found it difficult to keep up with their banter so I just kept myself to myself most of the time.

Not all the girls working on the game were like that, of course, and I was always happier in the company of girls who, like me, saw being on the game as a means to an end rather than a normal lifestyle. I guess most of them were kidding themselves when they said they were only going to do it for a few years, assuring anyone who would listen that it was just until they had made enough money to buy a house or establish themselves in some other business, but at least they still held out hope of attaining a better life. Most of the girls I was working with in the sauna only ever lived from day to day and gave most of their money away to the men who pimped for them. I didn't want to be part of their scene, I just wanted to make enough money to pay the bills and be able to continue with my normal life.

There was a CCTV camera on the door of the sauna so we could always see who was ringing the bell before letting them in. I had been working there a few weeks when I heard the bell and glanced at the screen as usual only to see one of my brother's closest friends standing there, nervously waiting to be let in. In that split second I realised how careless I had become. Just like when I had walked openly around the city with Aman, I had allowed the fact that nothing had gone wrong so far to lull me into a false sense of security. If one of the other girls had let him in without me knowing and he had seen me there he might well have let Ali know and I would either have had to go on the run for the rest of my life or risk being beaten to death, becoming another anonymous statistic in the missing persons files. The moment I saw his face on the screen I ran into the kitchen to hide, letting the other girls see to him. The moment he had disappeared upstairs I left the building with my heart still pounding.

That night I lay awake imagining what might so easily have happened. By that stage I couldn't think of anything else I could do to make enough money to meet all my needs, and I couldn't consider giving up working. I suppose in a way I had become as hooked on the money as Ali was on drugs and Asif on clubbing, and my mother was on sending money back to the people from her past life. I realised that if I was going to continue I had to make a radical change to the way I worked because sooner or later I was going to end up being caught, just as I had been with Aman. The next day I packed my bags and travelled to a new city at the other end of the country, which one or two other girls had told me was booming. I told my family that my boss needed me to work for him in new projects that he was setting up around the country. None of them ever showed the slightest bit of interest in my career, never asked me any questions, so lying to them was not hard.

Over the next few years I would work in a number of different cities. The first thing I found was that there was a big difference in the prices that girls could charge in different places. In some poorer areas there were girls providing services for as little as twenty pounds a time. In another city I found a sauna where they charged much higher prices and would allow the girls to stay overnight for twenty pounds, which meant I didn't have to pay for a flat or a hotel and I was available to work whenever I felt like it. When I went there for my initial interview they told me it would be possible to make between one and two thousand pounds a week. That sounded perfect and I agreed to join them immediately, thinking that if I worked hard there I could clear all the family's debts within a couple of years and would then be able to get out of the business.

When I flew into the local airport for the first time a car was sent from the sauna to pick me up, making me feel even more optimistic and not a little important as I was whisked straight into the city centre. There were between ten and fifteen very attractive, thin girls waiting for clients when I arrived and it was all set up as a sort of imitation of the famous Playboy Mansion in America, very luxurious and expensive-looking. The clients would walk into the lounge, where the girls were all scattered around like models, wearing almost nothing, usually just underwear and high heels, and they would pick who they wanted to take upstairs. I wasn't that comfortable at the idea of sitting around in my underwear.

'Can I wear dresses?' I asked the manager.

'Sure,' he shrugged, 'but the more revealing your outfit the more customers you are going to attract.'

He was right. As the customers came and went I hardly ever got picked and ended up making about a hundred and fifty pounds in the whole week, which didn't even cover the cost of my flight. I could see that the other girls were doing well, attracting one customer after another, and my confidence sank lower and lower each time a client walked past me with his eyes fixed on some other scantily clad little body. I felt as if I was the unattractive one again, just like Mum had always told me I was when I was young. It was bad enough feeling guilty for what I was doing, without feeling rejected and ugly at the same time.

Some of the other girls were also willing to 'specialise', which meant doing it without condoms or allowing anal penetration, and I still wasn't prepared to do any of that, which also limited my earning power. I was surprised at the risks the other girls were willing to take. They were all pretty enough to attract men without any extras and I couldn't understand why they felt they needed to put themselves in so much danger just to make a few extra pounds. They must have been even more desperate for money than I was. I know one or two of them had drug habits to fund and I understood from my experience with my brother how expensive that could be.

'Don't you do oral "without"?' one of the other girls asked me in surprise one day, probably feeling sorry for me because I wasn't getting as many customers as she was.

'I just couldn't do that,' I admitted.

'It's not that bad,' she said, as if trying to coax me into jumping into a cold swimming pool. 'Just swill your mouth out with mouthwash afterwards.'

'No,' I said. 'I know I'm really desperate, but I couldn't do that.'

There was another Indian girl in that establishment and I think my face was prettier than hers, but she had a perfect size eight figure and paraded around in her underwear all the time, which meant she was in much more demand. The clients I did get, however, all said they liked the fact that I had a fuller figure, so I knew there was a market for me if I was in the right place. I decided I should go back to working in flats but in this new city. I bought a local paper and rang a woman who was advertising for girls. She sounded very pleasant on the phone and so I went round to see her. She was so encouraging and enthusiastic when we met, assuring me that I would do very well with her clients, that she lifted my confidence right back up and I left the sauna the same day to move into the flat. She even allowed me to stay for free as long as I paid her twenty pounds for each client, plus fifty pounds a day to the maid.

Realising that I had to offer a few extras, even if I wasn't willing to 'specialise', I bought some sex toys, which I could charge the clients more for, and stocked up on blue movies which they could watch while we were together. Clients would ask for specific things in the movies. 'Have you got any with black girls in?' one would ask. Or, 'Have you got one featuring Asian girls?' I used to keep a dozen or so in the flat for them to choose from.

The first time I went into a sex shop I felt very embarrassed, but the woman behind the counter was so helpful and matter-of-fact about everything I soon lost my inhibitions and it felt just like buying any other kind of supplies. I got to know one shop so well I would ring up and the guy would drop round several videos at a time for me to try out, charging me thirty quid for a selection of six.

The woman with the flat had been right, within a few days of being there I was regularly servicing as many as a dozen clients a day. Some of them wanted to be dominated and I didn't mind doing that. It actually helped me to vent some of my own frustration in the process, although some of them wanted to be really hurt, which I didn't like doing. To be given permission to take a little bit of revenge for all the things that men had done to me through my life was great, especially as I could charge twice as much without having to have any sex with them at all, since they would usually want to satisfy themselves once I had finished tying them up or beating them. There was one man who even liked to have hot wax poured over his genitals, which I was perfectly willing to do for him, although I couldn't quite see the attraction myself. In one week I made six grand in just four days. It seemed I had found a profitable niche market and I began to think that I was finally getting somewhere.

Becoming more confident, I decided to cut out the middleman and hire my own flat so I didn't have to share the money I earned with anyone else. Once again I calculated that if I worked as hard as I could for just another year or two, I should be able to make enough money to pay the loan sharks off once and for all. One of my clients, who had become very friendly, helped me to find a suitable flat and to place my own ads in the local papers. I bought an answering machine so that I didn't even need a receptionist. Now I was my own boss and that was a good feeling, although I missed the company of having someone working in the flat with me, someone to chat to between clients, someone I could tell anything to, someone whom I might be able to laugh with now and again. A lot of the receptionists I had worked with had been very experienced in the business and I had learned a lot from them, like the first time someone rang up and asked if I did 'water sports'.

I hadn't got a clue what the man was talking about, but the receptionist knew exactly what he was asking for.

'He wants you to wee on him,' she said, as if it was the most normal thing in the world.

'You're joking.' I was having trouble taking this in. It had never occurred to me that anyone would want that. It sounded more like a torture than a turn-on.

'He'll pay the going rate,' she said, 'just make sure you have a bit of notice before he comes so you can drink a few glasses of water.'

I was soon to discover that a surprising number of people like that sort of thing, some even like being pooed on and are willing to pay for the privilege.

There were advantages to being on my own for at least

part of the day. Although I didn't have the companionship of the receptionists at least if I woke up in the morning feeling tired and not wanting to work I could just ignore the answering machine messages and go back to bed. The phone was constantly ringing if I left it on the hook, but I had discovered that if potential clients liked the sound of me from the ad they would always ring back if they didn't manage to get me first time. A lot of the calls were complete time-wasters anyway, men just wanting to masturbate while they talked to me. Some mornings it was simply too much effort to psyche myself up to put on the face and the act that the clients expected to see.

Often what would spur me into action would be a call from Mum, regaling me with some new horror story from home that was going to need more money to sort out. Ali would have run up another drug debt and Asif would need money to live, or one of them would have another fine to pay, or someone would have died in Lahore, or she or Dad would need some expensive medical treatment. By the end of the phone call I would feel no less depressed at the thought of having to sell my body again, but I would at least have a goal in mind, an amount of money that I now needed to earn by the end of the day, and focusing on that would get me through the next ten or twelve hours.

While I was earning so well I wanted to try to save some of the money and not let Mum's debts swallow it all, so I took out a mortgage and bought myself a nice little house not far from where I had been living with Karen. Everyone I talked to told me that owning 'bricks and mortar' was a good investment, but then none of those people realised quite how many other overheads I already had because of my family. By taking out a mortgage I had merely added to the debts that were forcing me to keep working every hour that I could. Initially, however, I was so excited to own my own home and to be earning enough to pay for it that I didn't think about how I was ever going to be able to give up the game now that I had interest payments of my own to meet as well as Mum's.

As I got ready for work each morning I would be talking to myself all the time, encouraging myself as I went through the routine of showering and putting on lotions and perfume and make-up, piling my hair up on top of my head, wriggling into skimpy little outfits and heels. Anyone listening in would have thought they had stumbled across a mad woman.

At the end of the day, whether I had reached my target or fallen short of it, I would be back in the shower trying to wash away the smells of the day before ringing home to talk to friends and family as if I had just had a normal day at a normal catering job, not able to tell them anything about how I was really feeling, not able to share the burden with anyone. I had chosen my path and I knew I had to walk it on my own whatever happened.

Most evenings I would then go round the corner to buy myself a sandwich or a tin of beans and the rest of the night would be spent staring at the television, flicking through the channels, trying to distract myself from dwelling on what I had been doing all day, trying to think of other things.

Although I had one or two sinister-looking clients in the years that I worked in that city, they were in the minority. Most of the men were very nice and polite and not too unpleasant to look at or touch. I still never told anyone that I was from Pakistan, always describing myself as Indian. I was constantly fearful that other Pakistanis might see my ads and if they thought I was a Muslim girl they might come round and do my brothers' job for them, beating or killing me as a punishment for dishonouring their religion and making a mockery of their beliefs. To any devout Muslim man I had turned myself into the lowest of the low.

One of my neighbours must have noticed how many cars were parking outside on the private gravel area that surrounded the flats and seen a variety of men coming and going every half hour or so. I hadn't realised anything was wrong until one of my clients rang me an hour or two after he had left the flat.

'The police are watching your place,' he told me.

'How do you know?' I asked, a terrible dread running

through me at the thought of being exposed.

'They stopped me as I came out. They're in a car outside. They asked a load of questions. Someone has complained that you're running a brothel. They wanted to know what I'd been doing in there.'

'What did you tell them?'

'I told them I just wanted a shag and they asked me how much I'd paid and took my car registration number and that was it. I think they will be paying you a visit.'

Sure enough there was a tapping at the door about twenty minutes later and when I went to open it I found a policeman and woman on the doorstep. They introduced themselves.

'We've had a complaint that there's a brothel being run on these premises,' the woman said.

I didn't deny anything; there didn't seem much point if they had already talked to one of the clients, so I asked them in.

'Is it just yourself working here?' she asked as she looked around curiously.

'Yes, this is my flat,' I said. 'I live and work on my own here.'

They were very friendly and didn't seem to have any objections to what I was doing.

'To be honest,' the policewoman said once I'd answered all her questions, 'we understand you're just trying to earn a living and we'd rather have you working in here where it's reasonably safe than out on the streets. It would only be a brothel if there was more than one of you working on the premises. You're not doing anything illegal here.'

'What about the complaint then?' I asked.

'The complaint was about a brothel,' the policeman said, 'and I don't see one of those, so you're all right.'

'If you ever have any problems with clients,' the policewoman added, giving me a card with a telephone number on it, 'just call us and we'll be happy to come and help.'

It seemed I now had the protection of the law, but somehow it didn't make me feel any better about myself or about the things I was doing. The only compensation I had for my bad conscience was the money I was making for the family.

16

Relationships

I had three regular customers who started to come back every week. One was a nice guy in his twenties with a young family; another was in his early fifties and behaved a bit like he was my father. He was the one who had helped me get the flat and set up on my own. He started off coming once a week, then twice, then he would bring a bottle of Archers for me, a bottle of vodka for himself and we'd sit down for a drink and a chat sometimes without even having sex. He was married with children too, like so many of my clients. Next he started bringing takeaway meals round to share with me on a Friday night, and I actually found myself looking forward to his visits. Even when he was due to come over for sex he would always ring first to see if I needed him to bring anything with him, and he would never let me pay him back for anything he bought for me. He would often make thoughtful little gestures. If he noticed that my perfume was running low for instance, and I was addicted to Allure at that time, he would turn up with a new bottle as a present. Or if he had noticed his wife buying something for herself, like a new sort of body scrub, he would go out and buy one for me too.

Pete, my third regular, was a bit younger, probably still in his forties, quite short, with lots of personality and chat. I liked him immediately. The first time he came for a booking he only stayed for half an hour, but the next week he phoned again.

'Are you busy today?' he asked.

'I'm afraid I am,' I said.

He tried again the next day and booked an hour of my time. He was full of flattery when he arrived and told me he was going to recommend me to one of his friends, which I thought was nice of him. Recommendations were always the best way of getting new clients. I always tried to be polite to all the men who came to see me because I knew most working girls didn't bother. I had a theory that they would treat me with more respect if I did the same for them.

'How about I take you on a shopping trip?' he suggested one week when he saw how little food I had in the flat. I was quite happy to take him up on the offer, and our shopping trips then became regular weekly dates, with him picking me up in his car and taking me off to a supermarket and paying for anything that took my fancy, sometimes suggesting new things I should try, popping them into my trolley as we went around the shelves together almost like a normal couple.

Soon he was offering to pay for my flights up and down from home and if I was staying over at a weekend and didn't go home he would pick me up and take me out for the day sightseeing around the area. It was beginning to feel as if we were in a relationship, although he was always happy to pay for my time. When Christmas came round he took me out on a giant shopping spree and spent a couple of thousand pounds on clothes and shoes and make-up.

'It's nice to see a smile on your face,' he said when I tried to thank him for his generosity. He genuinely seemed to want to please me and it was nice to get so much attention from a man for a change. It was a million miles from going shopping in Lahore and having Ahmed cross-examining me about every rupee I had spent.

The days out with Peter started to run on into evening meals and then he began wanting to stay over for the night, which was all fine to start with because I really liked having the company and he was always happy to pay for my time, but then he started to become a little possessive. He didn't like me entertaining other customers, and he started turning up unannounced when I was working, hammering on the door and shouting that he wanted to see me, which made things very difficult. Or he would be banging on the door at two in the morning, waking me up and demanding to come in. Sometimes if I had a client with me he would wait outside until he saw the man go, and then he would burst in and demand to book me for the rest of the day.

'I don't want you going with other men,' he told me, 'I want you for myself.'

'But I have to work,' I explained. 'I need the money.'

'Why do you need so much?' he asked.

'My parents owe money to loan sharks,' I explained, 'and the debt has gone up to over a hundred thousand pounds.'

'A hundred thousand?' He was obviously shocked. 'How did that happen?'

'I've been paying it back whenever I can,' I said, 'but I never seem to be able to pay all of it and the interest just keeps building every week.'

When I said it out loud like that it made me realise just how serious the situation was becoming. Most of the time I only thought of how much we owed that week or that day, the overall sum being too enormous to even contemplate. It was that same inability to see the big picture that had got Mum into trouble in the first place. I think to start with Peter was worried that I might be making the whole story up just to get money out of him, but as the weeks passed he got to know me better and asked me more questions and I could tell he was starting to believe me.

As he grew to trust me he told me more about himself. He owned a huge network of garages and was obviously extremely wealthy. He had a wife, and three children all of whom were at private schools. He suspected his wife of having an affair and that was how he justified seeing me, as an act of revenge. He even took me to their home for sex sometimes. It was the biggest mansion I had ever been in, with a huge sweeping staircase and marble hall and a drive-way filled with expensive cars. He was always very nice to me but his possessiveness was becoming increasingly worrying. I couldn't imagine how our relationship could end happily unless he lightened up and allowed me to have my own life.

Pete was with me in the car one day when I received a panic-stricken call from Mum. She was shouting hysterically down the phone and it was obvious she was deeply frightened. Pete, who was driving at the time, could hear much of what she was saying even though he couldn't understand a word of it and had to have me translating. Mum was so beside herself she didn't even realise I was relaying her story to a third party. The loan sharks had been round while she was on her own, she told me, and they had threatened to burn the house down and had pushed her around.

'You'll have to pay them off, you know,' he said once I managed to calm her down enough to allow me to hang up. 'They won't give up till you do.'

'I know,' I said. 'But even if I sold everything I possess I still wouldn't have anything like enough to clear the debt in one go, and if I don't do that the interest starts to build again. It's like a giant black hole which just keeps getting bigger and bigger.'

'I'll give you the money,' he said. 'Give me your banking details and I'll have it transferred to you tomorrow.'

I don't think I believed it was possible that anyone would do such a thing for me. I was very moved but it still made me uncomfortable. I knew I had no choice but to accept the offer, even though it meant giving him all my personal details when I was already nervous about how persistent and possessive he was becoming about me. A few days later the money arrived in my account and the next time I went home I was able to pay the debt off once and for all. I could see the loan sharks were shocked that I was able to get my hands on so much money in one go. They were obviously suspicious to start with, assuming I was trying to con them in some way, but once they had satisfied themselves that the money was real they went off looking very pleased with themselves. I told Mum and Dad that I had been investing in property, which was booming at the time, and that I had just sold a flat for cash. That, I told her, was how I was able to get hold of such a large lump sum.

Even with the debt paid off I was still left with the normal running costs of the family and my own overheads, but for a while it felt as if an enormous weight had been lifted from my shoulders. Mum didn't seem that impressed. I don't know if she ever truly realised how enormous the debt had become. I could tell that Dad was relieved and grateful, although he didn't say very much. I suspect he was embarrassed to think that one of his children had had to come to his rescue.

On the days when I was back at home and resting, I had actually managed to start a normal relationship with a man I had met locally who knew nothing about my working life, although no relationship could ever be completely normal when everything I told him about myself and my career had to be a lie. I had first met Zahoor while out in the clubs. Although he viewed himself as a good, religious man, he was not so strict that he wasn't willing to pick up a girl and go home with her. He had started out as one of my one-night stands but we stayed in touch after that. He was gorgeous to look at and there was a lot about him that reminded me of Aman. He smelled the same, and he had the same gentle ways of kissing me and pleasing me. Girlfriends told me they could tell that he really liked me and I began to feel that I might be falling in love again. I couldn't imagine that I could have a proper relationship with a man at the same time as working on the game, but Zahoor was very persistent and kept turning up on the doorstep at weekends in his best suit, flowers in hand. It was hard to resist such dedicated courtship, even though he didn't have the money to be able to indulge me in the same way as my regular clients did. I tried to ignore all the downsides because I still liked the idea of having a proper relationship and a man to look after me, rather than me having to look after everyone else. I also wanted to show Aman and my family that I was able to find a man who would love me and want to take care of me. Although I enjoyed being independent in many ways, I was aware that in the community I came from a woman on her own was someone to be pitied, and I didn't like the thought that anyone might be pitying me.

When we first met he had a job in a factory. He was earning just enough to make it feasible that he could consider marriage and supporting a family, although he wouldn't have been able to help me with all the expenses I had on behalf of my parents. Then the factory where he worked closed down, and he was left without a job. Things began to change. I don't know how hard he tried to get another job, but as the months went past it was obvious he wasn't succeeding and before long the only money that was coming into the relationship was mine and whatever he could get in benefits, which wasn't much.

He, like the rest of my family, accepted quite happily that I would disappear off to another city for four or five days a week as long as I came back home at weekends bearing gifts. I was still telling them all that I was working in catering and corporate entertainment and Zahoor was as uninterested as the rest of them in finding out any more. As long as I kept bringing in the money that seemed to be all that mattered to anyone.

By that time my parents and brothers had given up on hoping to influence my choice of husband. They weren't even very encouraging any more. They were probably nervous that if I did get married I might stop work and the money would dry up. They had allowed me to divorce Ahmed with hardly any protests, although I think Mum was probably still sending money to his family on the quiet when they asked for it. It seemed that if I wanted to marry Zahoor they were quite happy with that. I dare say they guessed that I was already seeing him even though we weren't married, but my brothers had bigger problems to worry about by then than the reputation and honour of their little sister, particularly as I kept my private life a discreet distance from the area where the family was known. I had become an adult woman to them all, a commodity with a different value. I was the only real breadwinner in the family, which was more important to them than my value as a potential bride to any uncle or cousin who might enquire. I was well aware, however, that although they had learned to be more tolerant about me having a relationship with a man, if they ever found out what I had been doing for a living over the previous few years it would have ignited all their old angers and prejudices. My brothers might sleep with prostitutes themselves but they would never tolerate one of the women in their family becoming one. I was still convinced they would kill me if they found out.

I was becoming increasingly fond of Zahoor, and I wanted to go on seeing him, but I was also becoming nervous that too many people would see us around town together and tongues would wag even more than they did already. Although I wasn't scared of my brothers physically attacking him as they would have done a few years before, I still cared about my reputation within the family. I didn't want to be seen as a loose woman, even though I was doing far worse things during the week than going out with Zahoor.

Although my parents seldom said anything about such matters to me any more, I didn't want them to have to suffer any more shame on my behalf than they had already. I wanted to show everyone in the family that although I had damaged my reputation by running away from the first marriage, my reputation was not irreparable. I still felt guilty about how much I had disgraced them in the past, and I began to think that if I married Zahoor then I would at least be protecting my reputation on the surface, despite the things that I was doing in secret. Zahoor had asked me several times to marry him and I had told him I wasn't ready. He was still holding out the hope that I would one day agree. Eventually I made up my mind and the next time he asked I said yes. He was so overjoyed I found myself being swept along by his optimism, actually convincing myself for a short while that this was a love match and that we stood every chance of being happy together.

I realise now that Zahoor must have believed he was marrying a rich woman. Because I could never tell him where the money came from all he saw was the nice house that I lived in at weekends and the nice car that I drove. The car was a BMW convertible, although it wasn't new and I had purchased it with a loan, just like the house. I had bought it one day on a whim when I was feeling low and wanted something to make me feel better about life, to take my mind off the guilt that was constantly gnawing away at the back of my head, to distract me from the feeling of being dirty.

It actually did make me feel better for a short time while I was driving around my home town in it, but the moment I parked it back at the house and got out the guilt was still there. That guilt was compounded by the fact that I had now started spending money on luxuries for myself like this car, when previously I had been convincing myself that I was only prostituting myself in order to support my family.

Most of the time it was too hard to think about what I

was really feeling, it was easier just to keep going, walking through life like a zombie, just getting on with things, doing what had to be done. If you know deep down that you are sinning but you feel you cannot stop because of your circumstances, then you can't afford to think too deeply about anything or you will go mad.

Because I wanted to have the sort of wedding I had always dreamed of, nothing like my first wedding in Lahore, I paid for everything myself. Once we had decided to go ahead and told our families, I bought the most beautiful red dress and lavish jewellery. I even paid for his outfit. I told myself that I was doing it to honour my parents; to make up for all the times I had disappointed them in the past. I wanted to be perfectly beautiful, if only for that one special day, and I hired a video company to film everything so that I would always be able to look back on that one idyllic time in my life, as if that would make up for everything else I was doing in secret. We had the henna ceremony at home and the next day I actually said my vows, unlike the first time in Lahore when the priest had hurried me through the whole thing as quickly as he could. We had a couple of hundred guests over the next few days and I could tell that there was a lot of whispering and exchanged looks of disapproval among the older women, all of whom must have known that I had run away from my first husband, and some of whom might also have known that Zahoor and I had been seeing each other for some time before the engagement.

Making love with Zahoor after the wedding felt completely different to anything that had happened to me before. It wasn't that the sex was any better or more enjoyable but the moment he entered me it felt halal and not haram. There was no guilt attached because this was my husband and I was there with him by my own choice. It wasn't long, however, before I was unable to keep thoughts from my other life out of my mind and the guilt began to gnaw away at me again.

A week after the ceremony I booked for us to go to a five-star hotel in Dubai for our honeymoon. I didn't mind paying for everything because it helped to lessen the guilt that I felt for the way in which I was earning the money and deceiving my new husband, but I was beginning to worry about how long I could keep the charade up if he didn't get a job and start bringing enough money into our family so that I could give up being on the game and take up some more respectable, if less well-paid work. Despite my worries I didn't nag him or put any pressure on him to help with the bills to start with. Perhaps I was too nervous about spoiling everything that we had together, or perhaps I had started to enjoy the feeling of being the breadwinner. Despite all the money I had been spending, I had managed to build up some savings and I was doing sums in my head all the time, wondering how long they would last us if a time came when I had to give up work.

It wasn't until after we were safely married that Zahoor confessed to me that he already had a wife and children. I was stunned. I felt totally betrayed, even though he assured me that he was planning to divorce her and that it had been an arranged marriage just like mine to Ahmed. I realised for the first time just how deeply hurt Mum must have felt when she first found out that Dad had been married before, but this was so much worse. I was angry with him for not telling me earlier, but I was willing to accept his word that he was going to end the marriage and that he was going to dedicate himself to me for the rest of his life. I didn't think I had any choice.

I had told Pete, my wealthy client, that I was getting married, and he seemed to find that as difficult to deal with as he found the fact that I had other clients. He started phoning me on my mobile when he knew very well I would be with Zahoor, which I didn't think was fair at all. I would never have phoned him when he was at home with his wife. In fact I never phoned him at all, I never needed to.

'I don't jeopardise your family life,' I told him crossly on one of these calls, 'so please don't jeopardise mine.'

For a few months I went back to my old routine of travelling up to work at the beginning of each week and coming home at the weekends, constantly doing calculations in my head, trying to work out a way that I could make enough money to give up. When I found out I was three months pregnant, however, I knew the decision had been taken out of my hands. I was going to have to stop working and stay at home. The thought of having sex with other men when I knew that I was carrying my first child was too terrible to even contemplate.

Giving up work, however, meant that I was going to have to break off my relationship with Pete. I explained to him what had happened but he wouldn't accept it. He kept calling and threatening to come round to tell Zahoor all about me. I pleaded with him to stay away, trying to make him understand that if my husband or brothers found out about me they would kill me.

'It's your choice,' he kept saying and in the end I knew I had to disappear from his life completely. I changed my mobile number and we moved house. I even changed my bank account because he had all my personal details after transferring the money for paying off the sharks. I managed to convince Zahoor that we needed a different house if we were going to start a family, and he didn't seem worried as long as I was paying and making all the arrangements. To get a quick sale I had to drop the price a lot and ended up having to increase the mortgage on our new home in order to be able to afford it, making our debt situation worse just as I was giving up work.

From the day I discovered I was pregnant I never went back to the city I had been living in part-time for the previous two years. I disappeared from that life as if I had never existed. Now I was simply a wife, a daughter, a sister and an expectant mother.

Zahoor was as excited as I was at the thought of having a baby and for a while it seemed as if we were finally going to be able to settle down and be a normal family. In my mind I convinced myself that we could survive on my savings for a few months, that Zahoor would find work and then, once the baby was born, I too could look for a part-time job that would fit in with being a mother. Zahoor was always talking about how he was going to find a job and work really hard and make lots of money to look after me. I always chose to believe that he would do what he promised, even though I could see with my own eyes that he wasn't actively looking for work, and could hear that many of the things he boasted he would do were completely impractical and would never happen. I wanted so much for him to be the provider so that I would never have to think about going on the game again that I allowed myself to be fooled by both our fantasies.

Living together in the same house for seven days a week turned out to be a lot harder than it had been when I had been travelling to another city to work five days at a time. It wasn't long before I realised that Zahoor was taking a lot of calls on his mobile that didn't seem to be from people I knew. I can't remember the exact moment when I started to become suspicious that he might be being unfaithful. It was more like a gradual realisation, I think. In my experience virtually all the men I knew cheated on their wives. I knew that my brothers did, and Aman had cheated on his wife with me. My father had betrayed his first wife by marrying my mother and virtually every client I had ever met had been cheating on a wife or partner by coming to my door. Even though I knew that, and despite everything I had done myself, I still couldn't face the thought of sharing my husband with another woman. Once the seed of doubt had been planted it quickly grew, and Zahoor reacted violently as soon as I started to question him about who was calling him. Furious at having to justify himself to a mere woman, he hit me hard in the face, knocking me to the floor. I lay there in shocked silence as I tried to piece together what had just happened to me. In all the time I had been working on the game, none of my clients had ever hit me.

My own conscience was so heavy from everything that I had been doing over the previous few years that my first thought was I deserved this punishment. It must, I reasoned, have been sent by God. I might not like being hit, but was it actually as bad as the things that I had been doing to Zahoor behind his back?

My next thought was fear for the baby I was carrying. I didn't think that one blow to my face was going to affect the foetus, but if I aggravated him any more he might become so incensed that next time he would punch or kick me in the stomach. I had heard enough stories of women being beaten by their men to know what an irate husband was capable of. I lay still and waited for his anger to pass while I worked out what to do.

In the following days I found out that the calls to his mobile were coming from other women he had been seeing while I was away, including his first wife, whose house he was visiting regularly, even staying over some nights. I felt hurt and betrayed, but I couldn't complain because I knew that I had been doing much worse. Our relationship remained volatile over the following months. I was desperate for him to give up the other women and be a good husband, while he was certain that I had no right to question his actions. I also wanted him to get a job because I could see that my savings were dwindling away far more quickly than I had expected and I was worried that the only way I would be able to pay for everything we needed once they were gone would be to go back on the game. All these worries were building up inside my head, but there was no one I could talk to about them. If my brothers ever found out what I had been doing they would kill me for sure. If Mum and Dad ever found out, the shame would kill them too. The stress of the debts and the continual trouble my Ali was getting into was already making Mum ill, and Dad had faded to a shadow of his former self. The last thing I wanted was to be the cause of any more grief for them.

Despite all these worries there were good times during the pregnancy too, and giving birth to my daughter, Jasmine, was the most wonderful experience of my life. I was so pleased when I was told that she was a girl because I felt that I would be able to give her the life that had been denied to me because of my upbringing. I would be able to protect her from all the pressures that men had put on women like Mum and me in the past, treating us like slaves or commodities to be bought and sold. When I held her in my arms in the hospital bed it felt like a new beginning and a ray of hope for the future. I didn't want to spoil the first few months of her life by worrying about anything, and so I pushed my head into the sand and concentrated on looking after her at the expense of everything else going on around me.

I stayed home and breastfed Jasmine for five months and tried to pretend that everything was going to be all right, even though I could see that new debts which my brothers were running up were putting pressure on Mum to find money once again. I knew that I now had nothing left to give her. It wasn't just that I had spent all my savings, I had also been using my credit cards too much and I could no longer pay them off in full each month. The interest was mounting up and I was slipping into the same trap as Mum. My greatest fear was that she would go back to the loan sharks and would become hopelessly trapped once more.

Zahoor was finding the restrictions of family life increasingly frustrating and violence was always bubbling just below the surface when he was around me, ready to burst through at the slightest provocation. Most of the time I managed to keep quiet, but every now and then I would speak up about something, trying to make him see my point of view, trying to persuade him to change his ways for Jasmine's sake. It nearly always resulted in him losing his temper. More and more often he was hitting me but I continued to hope that it was a phase we would be able to get through once our money troubles were over. I wonder now how many women allow abusive relationships to continue in the vain hope that things will get better, blaming some external factor like debt rather than laying the blame where it should be laid, at the feet of their violent men. The moment that I realised I couldn't continue was when he was hitting me one day with his right hand while holding Jasmine in his left hand. I knew then, as I frantically tried to pull my crying baby away from him, that I was fooling myself, and that the relationship could only get worse from then on. I realised that I would be endangering my daughter if I allowed it to continue. The last vestiges of my love for him drained away and all that was left was hatred and fear.

I rang the police that day, and when they came they were fully supportive of me. Zahoor was immediately apologetic and begged me not to press charges, but it was too late by then. I wanted the marriage to end so that Jasmine and I could be alone and safe together. I realised it had been a mistake to ever think that I could put my faith in any man. I wanted to be independent again, without having the faintest idea how I was going to achieve it.

17

Jasmine and Me

Once I had made the decision to end the marriage I knew I couldn't go back on it. Now that Zahoor had shown me how violent he could be I realised I had to accept that he would probably never change. Even if he could control his temper most of the time, there were bound to be moments when I, or Jasmine, would test his patience and we couldn't live our lives always being fearful of him exploding. I remembered all too clearly how my father would beat us for every tiny infringement of his rules when we were young, and I did not want Jasmine to have to experience anything like that from her father. I was certain that it would be better that she was brought up by a single parent than that she should live in fear every day of her childhood, forced into a blind and stupid obedience; just as it would be better for me to live alone than to be someone else's slave.

I had watched enough men like my brothers to know that Zahoor's life would almost certainly follow the same pattern of bullying and financial dependence on me. I had dreamed he would change once we were married and once our baby was born, but I could see now that that was all it had been, a dream. Now I had responsibility for another life I could no longer ignore the facts that were staring me in the face and kid myself that I could turn him into the sort of husband and father that I had hoped for. In some ways it was my fault for not being realistic about what Zahoor was capable of.

The police helped me to take out a court order banning Zahoor from coming near us. I missed him in many ways because I had loved him enough to marry him and I had never wanted my child to lose her father, but the alternative to that – living in an abusive relationship – was far worse. But now that I had Jasmine, and any fantasy that my husband was ever going to be able or willing to support us had gone, I had to be totally realistic about the future. The reality of my situation was that I was now on my own and deep in debt once more. I looked around for a job, but there was nothing on offer that would pay me anything like enough money to get me out of trouble. I decided I only had one option, which was to go back to the one profession that I knew I could make quick money at.

Mum, believing that I was travelling around the country working for a catering company, said she would be happy to help look after Jasmine for me if it meant that I would be bringing money into the family again, and so I set off to a new city to make the money I needed to get us out of trouble once more. To make it feel better, I told myself I would only need to do it for a limited time in order to make enough to get myself out of debt and then I would find something else; the same hopeless fantasy that so many sex workers survive on.

If having sex with strangers had been distasteful before, it was a thousand times worse now that I had Jasmine to think about. However hard I tried to concentrate on the work she remained constantly in my thoughts, her solemn little face hovering in my conscience all the time. Whenever the clients showed an interest in my breasts I could only think of how she had been suckling on them just weeks before. To me they seemed like my child's property and I hated the fact that strangers could stake a claim to them just because they had given me a handful of cash. In one terrible moment a client was sucking on my breast and it actually produced some milk. He seemed to think it was great, while I wanted to get him out of the flat as quickly as possible so that I could rush to the bathroom and throw up. But there was nothing I could say or do because it wasn't the client's fault. I was the one who had made the choice to sell my body again. I knew for sure now that I was a bad person and a bad mother and the weight of that knowledge sat heavily on my heart every hour of every day.

Not wanting to become involved with Pete again, I had

chosen to set up business in a bigger city this time, far away from him, a place where I would be even more anonymous than I had been before and where I thought there was a chance I could make a lot of money very quickly. By this time I had discovered the Internet as a way to advertise my services and I hired a firm to create a website, using photos of me in high heels and stockings. Stretched out in all the usual sexual poses and positions, I made sure they blocked out my face so that no one I knew who might be casually surfing the Net could recognise me. I had started afresh in so many different locations by then, I didn't think it would be a problem to do it again.

It is amazing how quickly the calls start coming when a new girl advertises. You only have to have been in a city a few days before the phone starts to ring and the customers begin to arrive. But these customers seemed to be different to the ones I was used to. Maybe it was because I was now in a big, anonymous city, or maybe it was because I had now had a baby and couldn't pretend for even a moment that I was doing this work of my own free will. Whatever the reason there seemed to be a more sinister air hanging around the clients as they came trooping through the door than anything I had experienced before.

I had rented a flat in a very posh area, thinking that would help to attract nicer, richer clients, but it was costing me nearly three thousand pounds a month. I was aiming high, charging two hundred and fifty pounds an hour, wanting to make a quick killing, but in fact the clients who turned up weren't anything like the wealthy residents I saw coming and going from the other flats around me in the elegant old Victorian block. I realised that in a really big city people move easily from area to area for services like the ones I was offering. Just as I had been amazed by how nice the clients were in the smaller city I had worked in before having Jasmine, I realised again that I had completely misjudged this latest move. Every moment that I spent in that flat I was enveloped in depression and eaten up with a painful physical longing to be back with Jasmine. I'd had to shake Pete off because he was so possessive, but I now dreamed of finding new clients as nice and considerate as he had been. Although it was worrying to have clients in love with you, it had its good sides too. To know that I was just one more anonymous girl for rent amongst thousands in a city where I had not a single friend was not a good feeling.

There was one client in particular whose visits brought home to me how low I had now sunk. He told me that he was a butcher, instantly bringing to mind Ahmed's bloodstained clothes and rough hands. Once I had undressed for him and lain down as requested, he pulled my legs apart with his thick fingers, using the crudest words imaginable to describe what he saw and how much he wanted to eat it. I felt as if I was one of the carcasses that he spent his days chopping up for consumption. As that image came to mind it was all I could do to stop myself from screaming. It didn't matter how long I spent in the shower after he had gone, or how much perfume I sprayed over my skin, I couldn't remove the thought of myself as a lump of meat splayed out on the slab, being eaten by his ugly great mouth. I could picture Jasmine, left back at home in Mum's irritable care when I should have been cuddling her and looking after her and protecting her, and I couldn't stop crying.

Even when I was at home alone with Jasmine at weekends, which was the one place I wanted to be, I still found I was bursting into tears for no reason all the time. Just looking at Jasmine asleep in my arms could set me off, or seeing her smiling up at me. I was continually scrubbing at myself in the shower, not knowing exactly what I was trying to wash away. I couldn't bear to look into her little face sometimes when she stared up at me because I would feel as if she was reading my mind through my eyes, as if she knew everything I had been doing that week during the days when I should have been caring for her. In order to find the strength to leave her again after the weekend I would have to distance myself mentally, and that made me feel even more guilty, as if I was rejecting her. I wondered if perhaps that was why Mum always seemed so unloving with us when we were small. Because she knew she had to keep working just to stay afloat, she decided it was better that we learned to be separate from her as quickly as possible. Was I going to end up as bitter and unhappy as her for the rest of my life?

Somehow I kept going back to that big city flat for two whole years, but every day the pressures were building up inside my head. I felt that I needed to be alone all the time to try to sort out my thoughts and decide what to do to get myself out of the trap I had fallen back into. It became harder and harder to find the energy to pick up the phone and take bookings from clients. It took even more energy to put on a happy, bubbly act when they turned up on the doorstep and handed over their money.

I started to take the odd day off, just staying behind my locked door with the phone switched off, staring at the television, my mind a blank. I was doing less and less each week until eventually I was sitting there all on my own all week, like a mad recluse, unable to do anything and horribly aware that the debts were still piling up while I sat in the silent flat in a state of emotional paralysis. The rent kept on streaming out and no money was coming in. I could no longer even bring myself to do the continuous mental calculations that had kept me going before, because the sums didn't add up now and they just brought on panic attacks. I didn't bother to eat or look after myself properly.

It was almost as if I was committing a slow suicide by simply giving up on living.

Whenever I was driving to and from work it would occur to me how easy it would be just to turn the wheel and drive myself into the oncoming traffic, or off to one side and into a wall. Then I would jerk back to consciousness and think of Jasmine and what would happen to her if I left her alone. Mum was old before her time and had never really changed her views of the world or of how little girls should be raised. She would find bringing a child up full-time hard work and would be bound to be as strict with Jasmine as she had been with me. If I wasn't there to protect my little girl my brothers would be intervening and making decisions, and they would try to marry her off as soon as she reached her teens, which would mean she could end up with a husband like Ahmed or, worse still, she might end up living as I now was. That was an unbearable thought.

Dad's health was not good, but our relationship was the best it had ever been. He no longer tried to tell me what to do with my life. I knew now that he was proud of what I had achieved, even though he had no idea how I had done it and was unaware that I was letting it all slip away from me again. He no longer seemed to care about my two broken marriages. All he knew was that I had a good job and was making enough money to be able to support the whole family and live a comfortable lifestyle myself. I didn't discuss any details with him about the loans I was taking out, perhaps because deep in my heart I knew that I wasn't acting wisely. So many things were never talked about in our family.

He became very ill while I was working in the big city and had to go into hospital for an operation. I went in to visit him one evening after I had driven back and found him on his own in a side room. As I sat down next to his bed he put his hand on mine.

'I'm sorry for all I have done to you,' he said. 'I've not been a help to any of my children. You have got on with your life and stood on your own two feet and I have never helped you. I'm really sorry for that.'

'It doesn't matter what you did or didn't do, Dad,' I said. 'Whatever it was, you did it for a reason. I have forgiven you long ago for anything that happened when we were young.'

That night I went back home with Jasmine on my own, having picked her up from Mum's. There was a pile of bills on the doormat, all of them urgent, all of them beyond my means. During the course of the evening two people came to the door shouting about money my family owed them, demanding payment. There was nothing I could do except turn the lights out and pretend I wasn't there. I had no money to give them and no strength left with which to make any promises. Jasmine had fallen asleep in my arms as I sat in front of the television and I carried her upstairs to bed with me.

I couldn't sleep as all my worries went round and round in my head, the light from the streetlamp outside bathing the room in a pinky glow, despite the closed curtains. Everything seemed hopeless and I imagined how easy it would be to start a fire downstairs while Jasmine slept beside me. I imagined how I would come back upstairs and lie down beside her, waiting for the smoke to put us to sleep forever. She would never know anything about it, I reasoned, and both of us would be spared any more pain or worry. If her life was going to end up being like mine then I wanted to free her from it at the same time as releasing myself.

The longer I thought about it with my sleep-starved brain, the more it seemed like the only way to escape from the terrible life we were trapped in. If I took my own life and the life of my child, I reasoned, then God would have to forgive me for all my other sins. I would have paid him back and my tired soul would be able to rest for all eternity. I decided to do it.

As I went to get up I leaned across and kissed Jasmine on the cheek. She opened her eyes, although she didn't seem to really wake up, and her little hands grabbed my hair. She pulled my face down and kissed me on the lips.

'Mummy stay here, lie down,' she whispered, before her heavy lids closed again, her thick black lashes resting on her perfectly smooth little cheeks. She held me tightly, almost as if she knew what I had been about to do to both of us and was determined not to allow it. Staring at her beautiful, innocent, sleeping face, I couldn't believe that I had even thought for a second that it would have been the right thing to do. At that moment I had reached rock bottom and knew that I was going to have to change everything if I was going to survive and give Jasmine the protection she needed.

All over that weekend I started to lay plans, newly invigorated and excited to think what the future might hold. The next week I didn't go back to work, nor did I take Jasmine round to Mum's. Instead I took her to the mortgage company with me and informed them that I could no longer keep up the payments, telling them they would have to take the house back. They were surprisingly nice about it. I guess it happens to them a lot. Then I went to the council and confessed that I was homeless and needed help and a roof for Jasmine and me. I was going to start all over again from where I had been before I decided to take the advice of the clairvoyant.

The council acted quickly as there was a child involved, and found us a small flat in a run-down area not too far from where the rest of my family lived. Within a week I had sold my car and all the clothes in my wardrobe, including the designer bags and shoes that Pete and my other regular client had bought for me. The money didn't amount to much considering how much they had all cost, but at least it was some cash so that we could survive and put food on the table until I got myself a respectable job. It felt good to have finally rid myself of everything that had been earned with such bad money. I felt strangely cleansed.

As I packed up all my possessions to take to our new home I found my old sketchbooks stored away under the bed, containing all the drawings and paintings I had done in the days when I had hoped to be a fabric designer. I was surprised by how good and fresh they looked after so long. The following week, once Jasmine and I were settled, I put together a presentation portfolio and started to go round to every potential buyer in the city. It was hard to get people to see me at first and I dread to think what I must have looked like, having travelled to their offices on buses or on foot, obviously desperate for work, obviously nothing like the art-school graduates and fashion experts they were used to employing. But whenever I actually got through the door and opened my portfolio I was surprised by how positive the reactions were. One or two of them actually asked me to go away and design something specific for them. I was shocked. Why had I never done this before? Why had I taken so many wrong turnings and almost ended up killing myself before I made the simple decision to follow my original dream?

The only answer I can come up with is that I had no one to guide me or to give me the self-belief I needed. It wasn't my parents' fault, they knew no better. Just surviving in a foreign country had proved almost too much for them. The only way they knew to help their children had been to follow the example of hundreds of earlier generations, relying on religion and repressive discipline. They knew nothing about careers for women or how to go about getting them.

But things are going to be different for Jasmine and me. I am going to set her the best possible example and show her just what a young woman can achieve in the world if she sets her heart on it. Whatever has happened in the past I am determined that I will never disgrace her again.

Acknowledgements

I would like to thank my publisher, Carly Cook, my agent, Shaheeda Sabir at Curtis Brown, and Andrew Crofts for all believing that this book would work and for giving me the confidence to tell my story.